GED® TEST SKILL BUILDER:
REASONING THROUGH LANGUAGE ARTS (RLA)

NEW YORK

Cataloging-in-Publication Data is on file with the Library of Congress.

Printed in the United States of America

9 8 7 6 5 4 3 2 1

ISBN 978-1-57685-989-6

For information on LearningExpress, other LearningExpress products, or bulk sales, please write to us at:
    80 Broad Street
    4th Floor
    New York, NY 10004

Or visit us at:
    www.learningexpressllc.com

CONTENTS ▶

CONTENTS

INTRODUCTION ▶

This book is designed to help people master the basic reading skills and concepts required to do well on the GED® Reasoning through Language Arts test. Many people who are preparing for this particular GED® test have not been in a school setting for some time. This means reading skills have gotten rusty or have been forgotten altogether. Others may have been in a school setting, but have not mastered various essential reading skills. By focusing on basic reading skills, this book will give its readers a better grasp of key reading concepts.

As the GED® Test Skill Builder title suggests, this book is not designed to prepare people to take the GED® test immediately afterward. Instead, its goal is to provide the necessary foundation of reading skills required for the GED® Reasoning through Language Arts test. Without these fundamental skills, it would be difficult for a person to prepare for the test effectively, much less earn a passable score. However, once these basic reading skills are understood, a person is then on the right path toward learning the concepts needed to succeed on this particular GED® test.

About the GED® RLA Test

In previous versions of the GED® test, the Language Arts section was divided into two separate tests: Reading and Writing. The new GED® test combines these into a single test. Questions in this section will ask you to do things like identify the main idea or theme in a reading passage or determine the meanings of words within a passage. The RLA section also tests your knowledge of grammar, sentence structure, and the mechanics of language. Sharpening your reading and writing skills is important for the GED® test, and not only for the Reasoning through Language Arts section: The GED® Social Studies test and the GED® Science test also measure your ability to understand and communicate ideas through writing.

The Reasoning through Language Arts test will contain a number of reading passages, each 400 to 900 words in length. Approximately 75% of these passages will be nonfiction, and the other 25% will be fiction.

Because the new GED® test is all given on the computer, you will see a number of different question types that are more interactive than the usual multiple-choice questions.

Question Types

The traditional **multiple-choice** questions will still be the main type you will see on the RLA test, and each item will have four possible answer choices to select from. This is a change from previous GED® tests, which had five choices for each multiple-choice item. There is still only one correct answer choice for each item. This eliminates the possibility of answer choices such as "All of the above" or "Both A and B," and allows you to focus on selecting the one correct answer.

On the RLA test, all multiple-choice items will refer to a reading passage; each passage will be followed by six to eight items. The layout for multiple-choice items related to a passage will be split-screen—the passage will appear on the left, and the multiple-choice item will appear on the right.

The RLA test will also feature **fill-in-the-blank** items. For these, you will type the correct answer into a blank line or box. The blank may appear in the middle of a sentence, requiring you to complete the sentence, or it may appear after a question, requiring you to type the correct answer. Some fill-in-the-blank items may include several blanks in a sentence or passage, asking you to enter several responses.

Another question format new to the GED® test is the **drag-and-drop** item. Drag-and-drop items usually feature a split-screen area with drag tokens, which you can move around the screen, and drop targets, which are areas where the drag tokens can be placed. For these item types, you will click on and drag each

token to the correct drop target. For the RLA test, this might involve anything from arranging the events of a reading passage in order to moving paragraphs in a letter so that they make the most sense.

Drop-down items are similar to multiple-choice items, but they provide embedded drop-down menus within a passage. For these item types, you will click on each drop-down selection and choose the correct or best answer from the options listed. On the RLA test, the drop-down item will most likely be used to test your ability to edit a passage.

The Reasoning through Language Arts test also contains an **extended response** item, which is the GED® test's essay question. The extended response item features a split-screen area with a short reading passage on the left and a prompt or question followed by a response box on the right. The extended response item requires you find and use information from the reading passage (or passages) to answer the question in a well-thought-out essay. Your essay will ask you to analyze an issue and provide an opinion on what you have read.

How to Use This Book

In addition to this introduction, *GED® Test Skill Builder: Reasoning through Language Arts* also contains the following:

- **The LearningExpress Test Preparation System.** Being a good test taker can boost anyone's GED® test score. Many of the skills and strategies covered in this book will be familiar to anyone who has taken many multiple-choice tests, but there is a large difference between being "familiar with the strategy" and being "excellent at using the strategy." Our goal is to get you into that second category, and this chapter offers you the means to do so.
- **A Diagnostic Exam.** It's always helpful to see where your reading skills stand. Therefore, we

recommend taking the diagnostic test before starting on the content chapters. By taking the diagnostic test, you should be able to determine the content areas in which you are strongest and the areas in which you might need more help. For example, if you miss most of your questions on the nonfiction passages, then you know that you should pay extra attention when the book discusses the best ways to approach nonfiction passages.

The diagnostic test does not count for any score, so don't get caught up on how many you got right or wrong. Instead, use the results of the diagnostic test to help guide your study of the content chapters.

- **Content Chapters.** These chapters form the heart of the book. Here we cover the basic reading concepts discussed earlier. To help you understand all these ideas, every chapter has sample questions, helpful tips, and summaries, as well as explanations of the concepts being discussed. We recommend reading these chapters in order and not skipping around, as many of the concepts in the earlier chapters are built on in the later chapters.

- **Two Practice Tests.** Once you have a better grasp of the basic reading skills, the best thing to do is to practice those skills. Both our practice tests are designed to be similar to the real GED® Reasoning through Language Arts test in terms of question types and passage content.

Taking these tests under timed conditions will help you gain familiarity with taking a timed reading test, which can help you in your GED® test preparations. However, if you would prefer to work on the questions untimed in order to focus on mastering the basic concepts of the content chapters, that's not a bad idea, either. Either way is helpful preparation.

Preparing for any test takes time. While we understand that there are more enjoyable things to do than studying basic reading skills, the concepts contained in this book will be helpful to you not only during the GED® Reasoning through Language Arts test, but in your personal and professional life after the test as well.

Good luck, and good studying!

CHAPTER

1 ▶ THE LEARNINGEXPRESS TEST PREPARATION SYSTEM

aking any written exam can be tough. It demands a lot of preparation if you want to achieve the best possible score. The LearningExpress Test Preparation System, developed exclusively for LearningExpress by leading test experts, gives you the discipline and attitude you need to be a winner.

Taking the GED® Reasoning through Language Arts test is no picnic, and neither is getting ready for it. You want to earn the highest possible score, but there are all sorts of pitfalls that can keep you from doing your best on this all-important exam. Here are some of the obstacles that can stand in the way of your success:

- being unfamiliar with the format of the exam
- being paralyzed by test anxiety
- leaving your preparation until the last minute or not preparing at all
- not knowing vital test-taking skills: how to pace yourself through the exam, how to use the process of elimination, and when to guess

- not being in tip-top mental and physical shape
- messing up on exam day by having to work on an empty stomach or shivering through the exam because the room is cold

What's the common denominator in all these test-taking pitfalls? One word: *control*. Who's in control, you or the exam? The LearningExpress Test Preparation System puts you in control. In just nine easy-to-follow steps, you will learn everything you need to know to make sure that you are in charge of your preparation and your performance on this GED® test. Other test takers may let the exam get the better of them; other test takers may be unprepared or out of shape, but not you. After completing this chapter, you will have taken all the steps you need to get a high score on the GED® Reasoning through Language Arts test.

Here's how the LearningExpress Test Preparation System works: Nine easy steps lead you through everything you need to know and do to get ready for this exam. Each of the steps listed here and discussed in detail on the following pages includes both reading about the step and one or more activities. It's important that you do the activities along with the reading, or you won't be getting the full benefit of the system. Each step tells you approximately how much time that step will take you to complete.

Step 1.	Get Information	30 minutes
Step 2.	Conquer Test Anxiety	20 minutes
Step 3.	Make a Plan	50 minutes
Step 4.	Learn to Manage Your Time	10 minutes
Step 5.	Learn to Use the Process of Elimination	20 minutes
Step 6.	Know When to Guess	20 minutes
Step 7.	Reach Your Peak Performance Zone	10 minutes
Step 8.	Get Your Act Together	10 minutes

Step 9.	Do It!	10 minutes
Total time for complete system:		**180 minutes— 3 hours**

We estimate that working through the entire system will take you approximately three hours. It's perfectly okay if you work at a faster or slower pace. If you can take a whole afternoon or evening, you can work through the whole LearningExpress Test Preparation System in one sitting. Otherwise, you can break it up and do just one or two steps a day for the next several days. It's up to you—remember, you are in control.

Step 1: Get Information

Time to complete: 30 minutes
Activity: Read the Introduction to This Book

Knowledge is power. The first step in the LearningExpress Test Preparation System is finding out everything you can about the types of information you will be expected to know and how this knowledge will be assessed.

What You Should Find Out
The more details you can find out about the exam, the more efficiently you will be able to study. Here's a list of some things you might want to find out:

- What skills are tested?
- How many sections are on the exam?
- How many questions are in each section?
- How much time is allotted for each section?
- How is the exam scored, and is there a penalty for wrong answers?
- Can you write in the exam booklet, or will you be given scratch paper?

Step 2: Conquer Test Anxiety

Time to complete: 20 minutes
Activity: Take the *Test Anxiety Quiz* (later in this chapter)

Having complete information about the GED® Reasoning through Language Arts test is the first step in getting control of it. Next, you have to overcome one of the biggest obstacles to test success: *test anxiety*. Test anxiety can not only impair your performance on the exam itself, but it can even keep you from preparing properly. In Step 2, you will learn stress management techniques that will help you succeed on your exam. Learn these strategies now, and practice them as you work through the activities in this book so that they'll be second nature to you by exam day.

Combating Test Anxiety

The first thing you need to know is that a little test anxiety is a good thing. Everyone gets nervous before a big exam—and if that nervousness motivates you to prepare thoroughly, so much the better. It's said that Sir Laurence Olivier, one of the foremost British actors of the twentieth century, threw up before every performance. His stage fright didn't impair his performance; in fact, it probably gave him a little extra edge—just the kind of edge you need to do well, whether on a stage or in an examination room. At the end of this section is the *Test Anxiety Quiz*. Stop here and answer the questions on that page to find out whether your level of test anxiety is something you should worry about.

Stress Management before the Exam

If you feel your level of anxiety is getting the best of you in the weeks before the exam, here is what you need to do to bring that level down again:

- **Get prepared.** There's nothing like knowing what to expect and being prepared for it to put you in control of test anxiety. That's why you're reading this book. Use it faithfully, and remind yourself that you're better prepared than most of the people taking the exam.
- **Practice self-confidence.** A positive attitude is a great way to combat test anxiety. This is no time to be humble or shy. Stand in front of the mirror and say to your reflection, "I'm prepared. I'm full of self-confidence. I'm going to ace this exam. I know I can do it." Say it into a recorder and play it back once a day. If you hear it often enough, you will believe it.
- **Fight negative messages.** Every time someone starts telling you how hard the exam is or how difficult it is to get a high score, start reciting your self-confidence messages to that person. If the someone with the negative messages is you—telling yourself you don't do well on exams, that you just can't do this—don't listen. Turn on your recorder and listen to your self-confidence messages.
- **Visualize.** Imagine yourself sitting in your first day of college classes or beginning the first day of your dream job because you have earned your GED® test credential. Visualizing success can help make it happen—and it reminds you of why you're doing all this work in preparing for the exam.
- **Exercise.** Physical activity helps calm down your body and focus your mind. Besides, being in good physical shape can actually help you do well on the exam. Go for a run, lift weights, go swimming—and do it regularly.

Stress Management on Test Day

There are several ways you can bring down your level of test stress and anxiety on test day. They'll work best if you practice them in the weeks before the exam, so you know which ones work best for you.

You need to worry about test anxiety only if it is extreme enough to impair your performance. The following questionnaire will provide a diagnosis of your level of test anxiety. In the blank before each statement, write the number that most accurately describes your experience.

0 = Never
1 = Once or twice
2 = Sometimes
3 = Often

____ I have gotten so nervous before an exam that I simply put down the books and didn't study for it.
____ I have experienced disabling physical symptoms such as vomiting and severe headaches because I was nervous about an exam.
____ I have simply not showed up for an exam because I was afraid to take it.
____ I have experienced dizziness and disorientation while taking an exam.
____ I have had trouble filling in the little circles because my hands were shaking too hard.
____ I have failed an exam because I was too nervous to complete it.
____ **Total: Add up the numbers in the blanks.**

Understanding Your Test Stress Score

Here are the steps you should take, depending on your score. If you scored

- **Below 3:** Your level of test anxiety is nothing to worry about; it's probably just enough to give you that little extra edge.
- **Between 3 and 6:** Your test anxiety may be enough to impair your performance, and you should practice the stress management techniques in this section to try to bring your test anxiety down to manageable levels.
- **Above 6:** Your level of test anxiety is a serious concern. In addition to practicing the stress management techniques listed in this section, you may want to seek additional personal help. Call your local high school or community college and ask for the academic counselor. Tell the counselor that you have a level of test anxiety that sometimes keeps you from being able to take an exam. The counselor may be willing to help you or may suggest someone else you should talk to.

- **Deep breathing.** Take a deep breath while you count to five, hold it for a count of one, and then let it out on a count of five. Repeat several times.
- **Move your body.** Try rolling your head in a circle. Rotate your shoulders. Shake your hands from the wrist. Many people find these movements very relaxing.
- **Visualize again.** Think of the place where you are most relaxed: lying on the beach in the sun, walking through the park, or whatever relaxes you. Now, close your eyes and imagine you're actually there. If you practice in advance, you will find that you need only a few seconds of this exercise to experience a significant increase in your sense of well-being.

When anxiety threatens to overwhelm you *during* the test, there are still things you can do to manage your stress level:

- **Repeat your self-confidence messages.** You should have them memorized by now. Say them quietly to yourself, and believe them!
- **Visualize one more time.** This time, visualize yourself moving smoothly and quickly through the exam, answering every question correctly, and finishing just before time is up. Like most visualization techniques, this one works best if you've practiced it ahead of time.
- **Find an easy question.** Skim over the questions until you find an easy question, and answer it. Getting even one question answered correctly gets you into the test-taking groove.
- **Take a mental break.** Everyone loses concentration once in a while during a long exam. It's normal, so you shouldn't worry about it. Instead, accept what happened. Say to yourself, "Hey, I lost it there for a minute. My brain is taking a break." Put down your pencil, close your eyes, and do some deep breathing for a few seconds. Then, you're ready to go back to work.

Try these techniques ahead of time, and see whether they work for you!

Step 3: Make a Plan

Time to complete: 50 minutes
Activity: Construct a Study Plan, using Schedules A through D (later in this section)

Many people do poorly on exams because they forget to make a study schedule. The most important thing you can do to better prepare yourself for your exam is to create a study plan or schedule. Spending hours the day before the exam poring over sample test questions not only raises your level of anxiety, but it also does not substitute for careful preparation and practice over time.

Don't cram. Take control of your time by mapping out a study schedule. There are four examples of study schedules on the following pages, based on the amount of time you have before the exam. If you're the kind of person who needs deadlines and assignments to motivate you for a project, here they are. If you're the kind of person who doesn't like to follow other people's plans, you can use the suggested schedules to construct your own.

In constructing your plan, take into account how much work you need to do. If your score on the diagnostic test in this book isn't what you had hoped, consider taking some of the steps from Schedule A and fitting them into Schedule D, even if you have only three weeks before the exam. (See Schedules A through D on the next few pages.)

Even more important than making a plan is making a commitment. You can't review everything you've learned in middle or high school in one night. You have to set aside some time every day for studying and practice. Try to set aside at least 20 minutes a day. Twenty minutes daily will do you more good than two hours crammed into a Saturday. If you have months before the test, you're lucky. Don't put off your studying until the week before. Start now. Even ten minutes a day, with half an hour or more on weekends, can make a big difference in your score.

Schedule A: The Leisure Plan

This schedule gives you at least six months to sharpen your skills and prepare for the GED® Reasoning through Language Arts test. The more prep time you give yourself, the more relaxed you'll feel.

- **Test day minus 6 months:** Take the diagnostic test in Chapter 2, then review the correct answers and the explanations. Start going to the library once every two weeks to read books or information about successful reading strategies. Find other people who are preparing for the exam and form a study group.
- **Test day minus 5 months:** Read Chapters 3 and 4 and work through the exercises. Use at least one of the additional resources for each chapter as you read it.
- **Test day minus 4 months:** Read Chapter 5 and work through the exercises. You're still continuing with your reading, aren't you?
- **Test day minus 3 months:** Read Chapter 6 and work through the exercises.
- **Test day minus 2 months:** Use your scores from the chapter exercises to help you decide where to concentrate your efforts this month. Go back to the relevant chapters and reread the information. Continue working with your study group.
- **Test day minus 1 month:** Read Chapter 7. Then, review the end-of-chapter quizzes and chapter review boxes in Chapters 3 through 6.
- **Test day minus 1 week:** Take and review the sample exams in Chapters 8 and 9. See how much you've learned in the past months. Concentrate on what you've done well and decide not to let any areas where you still feel uncertain bother you.

- **Day before test:** Relax. Do something unrelated to the GED® test. Eat a good meal and go to bed at your usual time.

Schedule B: The Just-Enough-Time Plan

If you have three to six months before the test, that should be enough time to prepare. This schedule assumes four months; stretch it out or compress it if you have more or less time.

- **Test day minus 4 months:** Take the diagnostic test in Chapter 2 and review the correct answers and the explanations. Then read Chapter 3 and work through the exercises. Start going to the library once every two weeks to read books or information about successful reading strategies.
- **Test day minus 3 months:** Read Chapters 4 and 5 and work through the exercises.
- **Test day minus 2 months:** Read Chapter 6 and work through the exercises. You're still continuing with your reading, aren't you?
- **Test day minus 1 month:** Take one of the sample exams in either Chapter 8 or 9. Use your score to help you decide where to concentrate your efforts this month. Go back to the relevant chapters and reread the information or get the help of a friend or teacher.
- **Test day minus 1 week:** Review Chapter 7 one last time and take the other sample exam. See how much you've learned in the past months. Concentrate on what you've done well and decide not to let any areas where you still feel uncertain bother you.
- **Day before test:** Relax. Do something unrelated to the GED® test. Eat a good meal and go to bed at your usual time.

Schedule C: More Study in Less Time

If you have one to three months before the test, you still have enough time for some concentrated study that will help you improve your score. This schedule is built around a two-month time frame. If you have only one month, spend an extra couple of hours a week to get all these steps in. If you have three months, take some of the steps from Schedule B and fit them in.

- **Test day minus 8 weeks:** Take the diagnostic test in Chapter 2 and review the correct answers and the explanations. Then read Chapter 3. Work through the exercises in these chapters. Review the areas you're weakest in.
- **Test day minus 6 weeks:** Read Chapters 4 and 5 and work through the exercises.
- **Test day minus 4 weeks:** Read Chapters 6 and 7 and work through the exercises.
- **Test day minus 2 weeks:** Take one of the practice exams in Chapter 8 or 9. Then, score it and read the answer explanations until you're sure you understand them. Review the areas where your score is lowest.
- **Test day minus 1 week:** Take the other sample exam. Then review both exams, concentrating on the areas where a little work can help the most.
- **Day before test:** Relax. Do something unrelated to the GED® test. Eat a good meal and go to bed at your usual time.

Schedule D: The Cram Plan

If you have three weeks or less before the test, you really have your work cut out for you. Carve half an hour out of your day, every day, for studying. This schedule assumes you have the whole three weeks to prepare; if you have less time, you will have to compress the schedule accordingly.

- **Test day minus 3 weeks:** Take the diagnostic test in Chapter 2 and review the correct answers and the explanations. Then read Chapters 3 and 4. Work through the exercises in the chapters. Review areas you're weakest in.
- **Test day minus 2 weeks:** Read the material in chapters 5 through 7 and work through the exercises.

- **Test day minus 1 week:** Evaluate your performance on the chapter quizzes. Review the parts of chapters that explain the skills you had the most trouble with. Get a friend or teacher to help you with the section you had the most difficulty with.
- **Test day minus 2 days:** Take the sample exams in Chapters 8 and 9. Review your results. Make sure you understand the answer explanations. Review the sample essay outline in Chapter 5 and reread the end of the chapter review box.
- **Day before test:** Relax. Do something unrelated to the GED® test. Eat a good meal and go to bed at your usual time.

Step 4: Learn to Manage Your Time

Time to complete: 10 minutes to read, many hours of practice
Activities: Practice these strategies as you take the sample exams

Steps 4, 5, and 6 of the LearningExpress Test Preparation System put you in charge of your GED® test by showing you test-taking strategies that work. Practice these strategies as you take the diagnostic test, sample quizzes, and practice exams throughout this book. Then, you will be ready to use them on test day.

First, you will take control of your time on the GED® test. The first step in achieving this control is to understand the format of the test. The GED® Reasoning through Language Arts test includes 74 items ranging from multiple-choice to extended response prompts. The total time allotted for the RLA test is 150 minutes, which includes a 10-minute break. You will want to practice using your time wisely on the practice tests and chapter quizzes and trying to avoid mistakes while working quickly.

- **Listen carefully to directions.** By the time you get to the test, you should know how the test works, but listen just in case something has changed.

■ **Pace yourself.** Glance at your watch every few minutes and compare the time to how far you've gotten in the section. Leave some extra time for review so that when one quarter of the time has elapsed, you should be more than a quarter of the way through the section, and so on. If you're falling behind, pick up the pace.

■ **Keep moving.** Don't spend too much time on one question. If you don't know the answer, skip the question and move on. You will be able to go back to it later if you have time.

■ **Don't rush.** You should keep moving, but rushing won't help. Try to keep calm and work methodically and quickly.

Step 5: Learn to Use the Process of Elimination

Time to complete: 20 minutes
Activity: Complete *Using the Process of Elimination* worksheet (later in this section)

After time management, the next most important tool for taking control of your test is using the process of elimination wisely. It's standard test-taking wisdom that you should always read all the answer choices before choosing your answer. This helps you find the right answer by eliminating wrong answer choices. And, sure enough, that standard wisdom applies to this exam, too. Let's say you're facing a question that goes like this:

9. **Sentence 6:** I would like to be considered for the assistant manager position in your company my previous work experience is a good match for the job requirements posted.

Which correction should be made to sentence 6?
   a. Insert *Although* before *I*.
   b. Insert a question mark after *company*.
   c. Insert a semicolon and *however* before *my*.
   d. Insert a period after *company* and capitalize *my*.
   e. No corrections are necessary.

If you happen to know that sentence 6 is a run-on sentence, and you know how to correct it, you don't need to use the process of elimination. But let's assume that, like some people, you don't. So, you look at the answer choices. *Although* sure doesn't sound like a good choice because it would change the meaning of the sentence. So, you eliminate choice **a**—and now you only have four answer choices to deal with. Mark an **X** next to choice **a**, so you never have to read it again. Move on to the other answer choices. If you know that the first part of the sentence does not ask a question, you can eliminate answer **b** as a possible answer. Make an **X** beside it. Choice **c**, inserting a semicolon, could create a pause in an otherwise long sentence, but inserting the word *however* might not be correct. If you're not sure whether this answer is correct, put a question mark beside it, meaning, "Well, maybe." Answer choice **d** would separate a very long sentence into two shorter sentences and would not change the meaning. It could work, so put a check mark beside it meaning "Good answer. I might use this one."

Now, your question looks like this:

Which correction should be made to sentence 6?
X **a.** Insert *Although* before *I*.
X **b.** Insert a question mark after *company*.
? **c.** Insert a semicolon and *however* before *my*.
✓ **d.** Insert a period after *company* and capitalize *my*.

You've got just one check mark, signifying a *good answer*. If you're pressed for time, you should simply mark answer **d** on your answer sheet. If you've got the time to be extra careful, you could compare your check mark answer to your question mark answers to make sure that it's better. (It is. Sentence 6 is a run-on sentence and should be separated into two shorter, complete sentences.)

It's good to have a system for marking *good*, *bad*, and *maybe* answers. We recommend using this one:

X = bad
✓ = good
? = maybe

If you don't like these marks, devise your own system. Just make sure you do it long before exam day—while you're working through the practice tests and quizzes in this book—so you won't have to worry about it during the exam.

Even when you think you're absolutely clueless about a question, you can often use the process of elimination to get rid of one answer choice. If so, you're better prepared to make an educated guess, as you will see in Step 6. More often, the process of elimination allows you to get down to only two possibly right answers. Then, you're in a strong position to guess. And sometimes, even though you don't know the right answer, you find it simply by getting rid of the wrong ones, as you did in the previous example.

Try answering the questions on the *Using the Process of Elimination* worksheet. The answer explanations show one possible way you might use the process to arrive at the right answer. The process of elimination is your tool for the next step, which is knowing when to guess.

Step 6: Know When to Guess

Time to complete: 20 minutes
Activity: Complete *Your Guessing Ability* worksheet

Armed with the process of elimination, you're ready to take control of one of the big questions in test taking: *Should I guess?* The first and main answer is *yes*. Unless the exam has a so-called guessing penalty, you have nothing to lose and everything to gain from guessing. The more complicated answer depends both on the exam and on you—your personality and your *guessing intuition*.

The GED® Reasoning through Language Arts test doesn't use a guessing penalty. The questions you answer correctly earn one point each, and you simply do not earn a point for wrong answers. So most of the time, you don't have to worry—simply go ahead and guess. But if you find that a test does have a guessing penalty, you should read the next section to find out what that means for you.

How the Guessing Penalty Works

A guessing penalty really only works against random guessing—filling in the little circles to make a nice pattern on your answer sheet. If you can eliminate one or more answer choices, as just outlined, you're better off taking a guess than leaving the answer blank, even on the sections that have a penalty.

Here's how a guessing penalty works: Depending on the number of answer choices in a given exam, some proportion of the number of questions you get wrong

Use the process of elimination to answer the following questions.

1. Ilsa is as old as Meghan will be in five years. The difference between Ed's age and Meghan's age is twice the difference between Ilsa's age and Meghan's age. Ed is 29. How old is Ilsa?
   a. 4
   b. 10
   c. 19
   d. 24

2. "All drivers of commercial vehicles must carry a valid commercial driver's license whenever operating a commercial vehicle."
   According to this sentence, which of the following people need NOT carry a commercial driver's license?
   a. a truck driver idling his engine while waiting to be directed to a loading dock
   b. a bus operator backing her bus out of the way of another bus in the bus lot
   c. a taxi driver driving his personal car to the grocery store
   d. a limousine driver taking the limousine to her home after dropping off her last passenger of the evening

3. Smoking tobacco has been linked to
   a. increased risk of stroke and heart attack.
   b. all forms of respiratory disease.
   c. increasing mortality rates over the past ten years.
   d. juvenile delinquency.

4. Which of the following words is spelled correctly?
   a. incorrigible
   b. outragous
   c. domestickated
   d. understandible

Answers

Here are the answers as well as some suggestions as to how you might have used the process of elimination to find them.

1. d. You should have eliminated choice **a** right off the bat. Ilsa can't be four years old if Meghan is going to be Ilsa's age in five years. The best way to eliminate other answer choices is to try plugging them into the information given in the problem. For instance, for choice **b**, if Ilsa is 10, then Meghan must be 5. The difference between their ages is 5. The difference between Ed's age, 29, and Meghan's age, 5, is 24. Is 24 two times 5? No. Then choice **b** is wrong. You could eliminate choice **c** in the same way and be left with choice **d**.

2. c. Note the word not in the question and go through the answers one by one. Is the truck driver in choice **a** "operating a commercial vehicle"? Yes, idling counts as "operating," so he needs to have a commercial driver's license. Likewise, the bus operator in choice **b** is operating a commercial vehicle; the question doesn't say the operator has to be on the street. The limo driver in choice **d** is operating a commercial vehicle, even though it doesn't have a passenger in it. However, the driver in choice **c** is not operating a commercial vehicle but his own private car.

3. **a.** You could eliminate choice **b** simply because of the presence of the word all. Such absolutes hardly ever appear in correct answer choices. Choice **c** looks attractive until you think a little about what you know—aren't fewer people smoking these days, rather than more? So how could smoking be responsible for a higher mortality rate? (If you didn't know that mortality rate means the rate at which people

die, you might keep this choice as a possibility, but you would still be able to eliminate two answers and have only two to choose from.) And choice **d** is plain silly, so you could eliminate that one, too. You are left with the correct choice, **a**.

4. **a.** How you used the process of elimination here depends on which words you recognized as being spelled incorrectly. If you knew that the correct spellings were *outrageous*, *domesticated*, and *understandable*, then you were home free. Surely you knew that at least one of these words was wrong!

YOUR GUESSING ABILITY

The following are ten really hard questions. You are not supposed to know the answers. Rather, this is an assessment of your ability to guess when you don't have a clue. Read each question carefully, as if you were expected to answer it. If you have any knowledge of the subject, use that knowledge to help you eliminate wrong answer choices.

1. September 7 is Independence Day in
   a. India.
   b. Costa Rica.
   c. Brazil.
   d. Australia.

2. Which of the following is the formula for determining the momentum of an object?
   a. $p = mv$
   b. $F = ma$
   c. $P = IV$
   d. $E = mc^2$

3. Because of the expansion of the universe, the stars and other celestial bodies are all moving away from one another. This phenomenon is known as
   a. Newton's first law.
   b. the big bang.
   c. gravitational collapse.
   d. Hubble flow.

4. American author Gertrude Stein was born in
   a. 1713.
   b. 1830.
   c. 1874.
   d. 1901.

5. Which of the following is NOT one of the Five Classics attributed to Confucius?
   a. *I Ching*
   b. *Book of Holiness*
   c. *Spring and Autumn Annals*
   d. *Book of History*

6. The religious and philosophical doctrine that holds that the universe is constantly in a struggle between good and evil is known as
   a. Pelagianism.
   b. Manichaeanism.
   c. neo-Hegelianism.
   d. Epicureanism.

7. The third Chief Justice of the U.S. Supreme Court was
   a. John Blair.
   b. William Cushing.
   c. James Wilson.
   d. John Jay.

8. Which of the following is the poisonous portion of a daffodil?
   a. the bulb
   b. the leaves
   c. the stem
   d. the flowers

9. The winner of the Masters golf tournament in 1953 was
   a. Sam Snead.
   b. Cary Middlecoff.
   c. Arnold Palmer.
   d. Ben Hogan.

10. The state with the highest per capita personal income in 1980 was
    a. Alaska.
    b. Connecticut.
    c. New York.
    d. Texas.

Answers

Check your answers against the following correct answers.

1. c.
2. a.
3. d.
4. c.
5. b.
6. b.
7. b.
8. a.
9. d.
10. a.

How Did You Do?

You may have simply gotten lucky and actually known the answer to one or two questions. In addition, your guessing was probably more successful if you were able to use the process of elimination on any of the questions. Maybe you didn't know who the third Chief Justice was (question 7), but you knew that John Jay was the first. In that case, you would have eliminated choice **d** and, therefore, improved your odds of guessing right from one in four to one in three.

According to probability, you should get two-and-a-half answers correct, so getting either two or three right would be average. If you got four or more right, you may be a really terrific guesser. If you got one or none right, you may be a really bad guesser.

Keep in mind, though, that this is only a small sample. You should continue to keep track of your guessing ability as you work through the sample test questions in this book. Circle the numbers of questions you guess on as you make your guess; or, if you don't have time while you take the practice tests, go back afterward and try to remember which questions you guessed at.

Remember, on a test with four answer choices, your chance of guessing correctly is one in four. Keep a separate "guessing" score for each exam. How many questions did you guess on? How many did you get right? If the number you got right is at least one-fourth of the number of questions you guessed on, you are at least an average guesser—maybe better—and you should always go ahead and guess on the real exam. If the number you got right is significantly lower than one-fourth of the number you guessed on, you would be safe in guessing anyway, but maybe you would feel more comfortable if you guessed only selectively, when you can eliminate a wrong answer or at least have a good feeling about one of the answer choices.

Remember, even if you are a play-it-safe person with lousy intuition, you are still safe guessing every time.

is subtracted from the total number of questions you got right. For instance, if there are four answer choices, typically the guessing penalty is one-third of your wrong answers. Suppose you took an exam of 100 questions. You answered 88 of them right and 12 wrong. If there's no guessing penalty, your score is simply 88. But if there's a one-third point guessing penalty, the scorers take your 12 wrong answers and divide by three to come up with four. Then, they subtract that four from your correct answer score of 88 to leave you with a score of 84. Thus, you would have been better off if you had simply not answered those 12 questions. Then, your total score would still be 88 because there wouldn't be anything to subtract.

What You Should Do about the Guessing Penalty

You now know how a guessing penalty works. The first thing this means for you is that marking your answer sheet at random doesn't pay off. If you're running out of time on an exam that has a guessing penalty, you should not use your remaining seconds to mark a pretty pattern on your answer sheet. Take those few seconds to try to answer one more question right. But as soon as you get out of the realm of random guessing, the guessing penalty no longer works against you. If you can use the process of elimination to get rid of even one wrong answer choice, the odds stop being against you and start working in your favor.

Sticking with our example of an exam that has four answer choices, eliminating just one wrong answer makes your odds of choosing the correct answer one in three. That's the same as the one-out-of-three guessing penalty—even odds. If you eliminate two answer choices, your odds are one in two—better than the guessing penalty. In either case, you should go ahead and choose one of the remaining answer choices.

When There Is No Guessing Penalty

As previously noted, the GED® Reasoning through Language Arts test does *not* have a guessing penalty. That means that, all other things being equal, you should always go ahead and guess, even if you have no idea what the question means. Nothing can happen to you if you're wrong. But all other things aren't necessarily equal. The other factor in deciding whether to guess, besides the guessing penalty, is you. There are two things you need to know about yourself before you go into the exam:

- Are you a risk-taker?
- Are you a good guesser?

Your risk-taking temperament matters most on exams with a guessing penalty. Without a guessing penalty, even if you're a play-it-safe person, guessing is perfectly safe. Overcome your anxieties and go ahead and mark an answer. But what if you're not much of a risk taker, and you think of yourself as the world's worst guesser? Complete the *Your Guessing Ability* worksheet to get an idea of how good your intuition is.

Step 7: Reach Your Peak Performance Zone

Time to complete: 10 minutes to read; weeks to complete!
Activity: Complete the *Physical Preparation Checklist*

To get ready for a challenge like a big test, you have to take control of your physical, as well as your mental, state. Exercise, proper diet, and rest will ensure that your body works with, rather than against, your mind on test day as well as during your preparation.

Exercise

If you don't already have a regular exercise program going, the time during which you're preparing for an exam is actually an excellent time to start one. And if you're already keeping fit—or trying to get that way—don't let the pressure of preparing for an exam fool you into quitting now. Exercise helps reduce

PHYSICAL PREPARATION CHECKLIST

For the week before the test, write down what physical exercise you engaged in and for how long and what you ate for each meal. Remember, you're trying for at least half an hour of exercise every other day (preferably every day) and a balanced diet that's light on junk food.

Exam day minus 7 days

Exercise: _____ for _____ minutes

Breakfast: _____

Lunch: _____

Dinner: _____

Snacks: _____

Exam day minus 6 days

Exercise: _____ for _____ minutes

Breakfast: _____

Lunch: _____

Dinner: _____

Snacks: _____

Exam day minus 5 days

Exercise: _____ for _____ minutes
Breakfast: _____
Lunch: _____
Dinner: _____
Snacks: _____

Exam day minus 4 days

Exercise: _____ for _____ minutes

Breakfast: _____

Lunch: _____

Dinner: _____

Snacks: _____

Exam day minus 3 days

Exercise: _____ for _____ minutes

Breakfast: _____

Lunch: _____

Dinner: _____

Snacks: _____

Exam day minus 2 days

Exercise: _____ for _____ minutes

Breakfast: _____

Lunch: _____

Dinner: _____

Snacks: _____

Day before exam

Exercise: _____ for _____ minutes

Breakfast: _____

Lunch: _____

Dinner: _____

Snacks: _____

stress by pumping wonderful, good-feeling hormones called *endorphins* into your system. It also increases the oxygen supply throughout your body, including your brain, so you will be at peak performance on exam day.

A half hour of vigorous activity—enough to raise a sweat—every day should be your aim. If you're really pressed for time, every other day is okay. Choose an activity you like and get out there and do it. Jogging with a friend always makes the time go faster, as does running with an MP3 player. But don't overdo it. You don't want to exhaust yourself. Moderation is the key.

Diet

First of all, cut out the junk. Then, go easy on caffeine. What your body needs for peak performance is simply a balanced diet. Eat plenty of fruits and vegetables, along with protein and carbohydrates. Foods that are high in lecithin (an amino acid), such as fish and beans, are especially good brain foods. The night before the test, you might carbo-load the way athletes do before a contest. Eat a big plate of spaghetti, rice and beans, or whatever your favorite carbohydrate is.

Rest

You probably know how much sleep you need every night to be at your best, even if you don't always get it. Make sure you do get that much sleep, though, for at least a week before the exam. Moderation is important here, too. Too much sleep will just make you groggy.

If you are not a morning person and your test will be given in the morning, you should reset your internal clock so that your body doesn't think you're taking an exam at 3 A.M. You have to start this process well before the day of the test. The way it works is to get up half an hour earlier each morning and then go to bed half an hour earlier each night. Don't try it the other way around; you will just toss and turn if you go to bed early without having gotten up early. The next morning, get up another half an hour earlier, and so on. How long you will have to do this depends on how

late you're used to getting up. Use the *Physical Preparation Checklist* to make sure you're in tip-top form.

Step 8: Get Your Act Together

Time to complete: 10 minutes to read; time to complete will vary
Activity: Complete *Final Preparations* worksheet

You're in control of your mind and body; you're in charge of test anxiety, your preparation, and your test-taking strategies. Now, it's time to take charge of external factors, like the testing site and the materials you need to take the exam.

Find Out Where the Exam Is and Make a Trial Run

Make sure you know exactly when and where your test is being held. Do you know how to get to the exam site? Do you know how long it will take to get there? If not, make a trial run, preferably on the same day of the week at the same time of day as the real test. Note on the *Final Preparations* worksheet the amount of time it will take you to get to the test site. Plan on arriving 10 to 15 minutes early so that you can get the lay of the land, use the bathroom, and calm down. Then, figure out how early you will have to get up that morning and make sure you get up that early every day for a week before the test.

Gather Your Materials

The night before the exam, lay out the clothes you will wear and the materials you have to bring with you to the test. Plan on dressing in layers; you won't have any control over the temperature of the examination room. Have a sweater or jacket you can take off if it's warm. Use the checklist on the *Final Preparations* worksheet to help you pull together what you will need.

Don't Skip Breakfast

Even if you don't usually eat breakfast, do so on the morning of the test. A cup of coffee or can of soda doesn't count. Don't eat doughnuts or other sweet foods, either. A sugar high will leave you with a sugar low in the middle of the test. A mix of protein and carbohydrates is best. Cereal with milk and just a little sugar or eggs with toast will do your body a world of good.

Step 9: Do It!

Time to complete: 10 minutes, plus test-taking time
Activity: Ace the GED® Reasoning through
    Language Arts Test!

Fast-forward to test day. You're ready. You made a study plan and followed through. You practiced your test-taking strategies while working through this book. You're in control of your physical, mental, and emotional state. You know when and where to show up and what to bring with you. In other words, you're better prepared than most of the other people taking the GED® test with you. You're psyched.

Just one more thing. When you're finished with the test, you will have earned a reward. Plan a celebration. Call your friends and plan a party, have a nice dinner with your family, or pick out a movie to see—whatever your heart desires. Give yourself something to look forward to.

And then do it. Go into the test full of confidence, armed with test-taking strategies you've practiced until they're second nature. You're in control of yourself, your environment, and your performance on the exam. You're ready to succeed. So do it. Go in there and ace the test. And look forward to your future as someone who has successfully passed the GED® test!

Getting to the Exam Site

Location of exam site: _____

Date of exam: _____

Departure time: _____

Do I know how to get to the exam site?   Yes ___   No ___

If No, make a trial run.

Time it will take to get to the exam site: _____

Things to Lay Out the Night Before

Clothes I will wear   _____

Sweater/jacket   _____

Watch   _____

Photo ID   _____

Other Things to Bring/Remember

_____   _____

_____   _____

_____   _____

_____   _____

_____   _____

_____   _____

_____   _____

_____   _____

2 ▶ DIAGNOSTIC TEST

CHAPTER SUMMARY

This is the first of the three practice tests in this book based on the GED® Reasoning through Language Arts test. Use this test to see how you would do if you were to take the exam today.

This diagnostic practice exam is of the same type as the real GED® Reasoning through Language Arts test. It consists of 50 multiple-choice questions and one essay question. These questions test your skills in comprehension (extracting meaning), application (using information), analysis (breaking down information), and synthesis (putting elements together).

The answer sheet you should use for the multiple-choice questions is on the following page. Then comes the exam itself, and after that, the answer key. Each answer on the test is explained in the answer key to help you find out why the correct answers are right and why the incorrect answers are wrong.

Diagnostic Test

	a	b	c	d
1.	ⓐ	ⓑ	ⓒ	ⓓ
2.	ⓐ	ⓑ	ⓒ	ⓓ
3.	ⓐ	ⓑ	ⓒ	ⓓ
4.	ⓐ	ⓑ	ⓒ	ⓓ
5.	ⓐ	ⓑ	ⓒ	ⓓ
6.	ⓐ	ⓑ	ⓒ	ⓓ
7.	ⓐ	ⓑ	ⓒ	ⓓ
8.	ⓐ	ⓑ	ⓒ	ⓓ
9.	ⓐ	ⓑ	ⓒ	ⓓ
10.	ⓐ	ⓑ	ⓒ	ⓓ
11.	ⓐ	ⓑ	ⓒ	ⓓ
12.	ⓐ	ⓑ	ⓒ	ⓓ
13.	ⓐ	ⓑ	ⓒ	ⓓ
14.	ⓐ	ⓑ	ⓒ	ⓓ
15.	ⓐ	ⓑ	ⓒ	ⓓ
16.	ⓐ	ⓑ	ⓒ	ⓓ
17.	ⓐ	ⓑ	ⓒ	ⓓ

	a	b	c	d
18.	ⓐ	ⓑ	ⓒ	ⓓ
19.	ⓐ	ⓑ	ⓒ	ⓓ
20.	ⓐ	ⓑ	ⓒ	ⓓ
21.	ⓐ	ⓑ	ⓒ	ⓓ
22.	ⓐ	ⓑ	ⓒ	ⓓ
23.	ⓐ	ⓑ	ⓒ	ⓓ
24.	ⓐ	ⓑ	ⓒ	ⓓ
25.	ⓐ	ⓑ	ⓒ	ⓓ
26.	ⓐ	ⓑ	ⓒ	ⓓ
27.	ⓐ	ⓑ	ⓒ	ⓓ
28.	ⓐ	ⓑ	ⓒ	ⓓ
29.	ⓐ	ⓑ	ⓒ	ⓓ
30.	ⓐ	ⓑ	ⓒ	ⓓ
31.	ⓐ	ⓑ	ⓒ	ⓓ
32.	ⓐ	ⓑ	ⓒ	ⓓ
33.	ⓐ	ⓑ	ⓒ	ⓓ
34.	ⓐ	ⓑ	ⓒ	ⓓ

	a	b	c	d
35.	ⓐ	ⓑ	ⓒ	ⓓ
36.	ⓐ	ⓑ	ⓒ	ⓓ
37.	ⓐ	ⓑ	ⓒ	ⓓ
38.	ⓐ	ⓑ	ⓒ	ⓓ
39.	ⓐ	ⓑ	ⓒ	ⓓ
40.	ⓐ	ⓑ	ⓒ	ⓓ
41.	ⓐ	ⓑ	ⓒ	ⓓ
42.	ⓐ	ⓑ	ⓒ	ⓓ
43.	ⓐ	ⓑ	ⓒ	ⓓ
44.	ⓐ	ⓑ	ⓒ	ⓓ
45.	ⓐ	ⓑ	ⓒ	ⓓ
46.	ⓐ	ⓑ	ⓒ	ⓓ
47.	ⓐ	ⓑ	ⓒ	ⓓ
48.	ⓐ	ⓑ	ⓒ	ⓓ
49.	ⓐ	ⓑ	ⓒ	ⓓ
50.	ⓐ	ⓑ	ⓒ	ⓓ

Directions: Choose the *one best answer* to each question.

Questions 1 through 7 refer to the following excerpt from a novel.

Will Anne Miss Green Gables?

It was a happy and beautiful bride who came down the old carpeted stairs that September noon. She was the first bride of Green Gables, slender and shining-eyed, with her
(5) arms full of roses. Gilbert, waiting for her in the hall below, looked up at her with adoring eyes. She was his at last, this long-sought Anne, whom he won after years of patient waiting. It was to him she was coming. Was
(10) he worthy of her? Could he make her as happy as he hoped? If he failed her—if he could not measure up to her standards. . . .

But then, their eyes met and all doubt was swept away in a certainty that everything
(15) would be wonderful. They belonged to each other; no matter what life might hold for them, it could never alter that. Their happiness was in each other's keeping and both were unafraid.

(20) They were married in the sunshine of the old orchard, circled by the loving and kindly faces of long-familiar friends. Mr. Allan married them and the Reverend Jo made what Mrs. Rachel Lynde afterwards
(25) pronounced to be the "most beautiful wedding prayer" she had ever heard. Birds do not often sing in September, but one sang sweetly from some hidden tree while Gilbert and Anne repeated their vows. Anne heard it
(30) and thrilled to it. Gilbert heard it and wondered only that all the birds in the world had not burst into jubilant song. The bird sang until the ceremony was ended. Then it wound up with one more little, glad trill.

(35) Never had the old gray-green house among its enfolding orchards known a merrier afternoon. Laughter and joy had their way; and when Anne and Gilbert left to catch their train, Marilla stood at the gate
(40) and watched them drive out of sight down the long lane with its banks of goldenrod. Anne turned at its end to wave her last goodbye. She looked once more at her home and felt a tinge of sadness. Then she was
(45) gone—Green Gables was her home no more. It would never be again. Marilla's face looked very gray and old as she turned to the house which Anne had filled for years with light and life.

Adapted from L.M. Montgomery,
Anne's House of Dreams

1. Which of the following words best describes what Gilbert feels toward Anne?
   a. love
   b. respect
   c. gratitude
   d. nervousness

2. What happened when Gilbert's and Anne's eyes met?
   a. He wondered whether he was worthy of her.
   b. He wondered what their life would be like.
   c. He realized they were meant for each other.
   d. He thought Anne would miss Green Gables very much.

3. Based on the excerpt, what was probably the hardest change for Anne?
   a. becoming a wife
   b. saying goodbye to Marilla
   c. not being free to do what she wanted
   d. Green Gables not being her home any longer

4. Based on the excerpt, which description best characterizes the relationship between Marilla and Anne?

    a. Marilla felt tired from having taken care of Anne.

    b. Marilla raised Anne from childhood and cared about her.

    c. Marilla was sad that Anne left because she would have to leave, too.

    d. Marilla and Anne disagreed about Gilbert being a good husband.

5. Which of the following best describes what the author means when she says "this long-sought Anne" (lines 7 and 8)?

    a. Anne was no longer a young woman.

    b. Anne did not fall in love with Gilbert right away.

    c. Anne was patient with Gilbert.

    d. Anne had nearly married someone else.

6. Of the characters in this excerpt, whose inner thoughts are hidden from the reader?

    a. Anne

    b. Gilbert

    c. Marilla

    d. Mr. Allan

7. How does the bird's singing relate to Gilbert's and Anne's marriage?

    a. The bird's singing was distracting to those watching the service.

    b. The bird's singing mirrored the joy of the wedding service.

    c. The bird's singing seemed to suggest sad events in the future.

    d. The bird's singing was worrisome to the bridal couple.

Directions: Choose the *one best answer* to each question.

Questions 8 through 14 are based on the following passage.

Raymond Dean
Green Valley Farm
3421 Rte 32
Stone Ridge, NY 12430

Dear Mr. Dean:

(A)

(1) I am presently a student at ulster county community college and my field of study is agriculture. (2) I am studying all types of farming techniques, and only prefers organic methods for growing vegetables. (3) I have learned much about the latest techniques for growing food organically and I know that since you are one of the largest organic growers in the area, I will learn a great deal more from you and your employees.

(B)

(4) This is why I would like to apply for a summer position with your farm. (5) I hope to get a permanent job with you after I graduate. (6) I believe the experience of working with the Green Valley Farm professionals would, enhance my education greatly. (7) I want to let you know that I would consider an unpaid internship at your farm. (8) That is how anxious I am to work with you. (9) Maybe I could borrow some money from my parents or get a second job to support myself. (10) I am enclosing my resume as well as my references from teachers and a former employer.

(C)

(11) I first learned about your farm from a teacher. (12) He has high regard for your work. (13) He was suggesting that I write you and make this request. (14) I hope I will hear from you. (15) In the near future.

Sincerely yours,

Mark Tanzania

8. Sentence (1): I am presently a student at <u>ulster county community college</u> and my field of study is agriculture.

   Which is the best way to write the underlined portion of the sentence?
   a. ulster county Community College
   b. Ulster county community college
   c. Ulster County Community college
   d. Ulster County Community College

9. Sentence (2): I am studying all types of farming <u>techniques, and only prefers</u> organic methods for growing vegetables.

   Which is the best way to write the underlined portion of this sentence?
   a. techniques, so I prefer
   b. techniques which are
   c. techniques, but prefer
   d. techniques that don't prefer

10. Sentences (4) and (5): This is why I would like to apply for a summer position with your farm. I hope to get a permanent job with you after I graduate.

   Which is the most effective combination of sentences (4) and (5)?
   a. I am applying for a summer job, but I hope to get a permanent position.
   b. Applying for a job now in the hopes that you will hire me after I graduate.
   c. I would like to apply for a position with your farm, today, and then later after I graduate.
   d. I would like to apply for a summer position with your farm in the hopes of having a permanent job with you after I graduate.

11. Which revision would improve the effectiveness of paragraph (B)?
   a. move sentence (5) after sentence (10)
   b. move sentence (9) to the end of the paragraph
   c. remove sentence (6)
   d. remove sentence (9)

12. Sentence (6): I believe the experience of working with the Green Valley Farm professionals would, enhance my education greatly.

   Which correction should be made to sentence (6)?
   a. insert a comma after <u>professionals</u>
   b. replace <u>working</u> with <u>to work</u>
   c. change <u>believe</u> to <u>believed</u>
   d. remove the comma after <u>would</u>

13. Sentences (11) and (12): I first learned about your farm from a teacher. He has high regard for your work.

Which is the most effective combination of sentences (11) and (12)?

a. First I learned about your farm from a teacher he has high regard for your work.

b. I learned about your farm from a teacher who has high regard for your work.

c. My teacher has high regard for your work, I learned about your farm.

d. A teacher who has high regard for your work and I first learned about your farm.

14. Sentence (13): He was suggesting that I write you and make this request.

Which correction should be made to sentence (13)?

a. change <u>make</u> to <u>made</u>

b. change <u>you</u> and <u>make</u> to <u>you. Make</u>

c. change <u>was suggesting</u> to <u>suggested</u>

d. change <u>was suggesting</u> to <u>have suggested</u>

Questions 15 through 18 refer to the following excerpt from a short story.

Will He Appear on National Television?

"I think half the world has shown up for this audition." Gene was talking on his cell phone to his girlfriend. "I can't wait to perform. I know I'm in fine voice, and they are going to

(5) love the song I chose."

"Well, good luck. I will be thinking of you."

Although he sounded upbeat with his girlfriend, in truth Gene was anything but

(10) confident. He had staked so much on the audition, and he had no idea what the judges would really think of him. He realized for the first time that he was scared. Even so, he wanted to succeed so much he could almost

(15) taste it. Just imagine competing on national television. He took a long breath in. It was hard to believe he was actually going to perform for the judges.

He had arrived exactly at nine and had

(20) been in line for over three hours. He could hear his heart beating loudly. Right then, Gene heard his name being called. He went into the building and was ushered into the audition room.

(25) "Yes, I'm here," he answered.

Gene looked at the judges sitting at the table. They seemed bored and unimpressed.

"Well, what are you going to sing for us today?" one of the judges asked him. "Time

(30) After Time," Gene told him, his voice quavering a bit.

"Okay, let's see what you've got," said another judge who was tapping the table with a pencil.

(35) Gene felt a knot in his throat and didn't know if he could go on. He remembered what his voice coach told him: "Just take a moment before you start. Close your eyes. Take a deep breath, and then let go." Gene

(40)   closed his eyes and took a breath and then a
        sweet voice began emanating from his
        mouth. The judges seemed to disappear. He
        could have been anywhere. He was in his
        own world.

(45)   Suddenly it was over, and he stood in
        front of the judges feeling very alone and
        vulnerable. He could feel the sweat on his
        brow.

            "Well, that was a surprise," said the first
(50)   judge. "I never would have predicted that."

            "What do you think? Does he go
        through?" All four of the judges gave him a
        thumbs up. "You're in, kid," the first judge
        said. "Don't make us regret our decision."

(55)   "Oh, no, sir. You won't regret it," Gene
        said as he nearly skipped out of the room.

15. Based on the excerpt, what does Gene most
likely think about the audition?
   a. It will give him a chance to make a good
   living.
   b. It is something he had wanted to avoid.
   c. It is a chance for him to be discovered.
   d. It will make him famous in a short time.

16. When does the scene in this excerpt take place?
   a. early morning
   b. late afternoon
   c. early afternoon
   d. early evening

17. Which is the best description of Gene's
performance?
   a. a good try but not good enough
   b. a fine voice but without true conviction
   c. a bit slow to start but ultimately wonderful
   d. a showy voice but not much rhythm

18. What is the main effect of the author's use of
phrases such as "could almost taste it," "took a
long breath in," and "beating loudly"?
   a. to show how long Gene had been waiting
   b. to show that Gene was talented
   c. to show that Gene had been exercising
   d. to show how important the audition was to
   Gene

*Questions 19 through 25 are based on the following
passage.*

Gorée Island

(A)

(1) Europeans played a large part in bringing slaves to America from west africa.
(2) Because European countries sent out
explorers who sailed down the west coast of
Africa. (3) They came in contact with the
people there. (4) They traded with them,
but they also captures many of the people.
(5) These people were sent to the New World
where they became slaves. (6) Most of them
ended up working on farms and plantations.

(B)

(7) Some Africans were sent from Gorée, a
small island off the coast of what is now Senegal. (8) There are about nine and a half million people in Senegal today. (9) They stayed
in dungeons until the ships from the New
World came to take them to America and the
Caribbean. (10) Some Africans also profited
from the slave trade. (11) A group of free
African women, called *signares*, sold food to
the European traders for the enslaved people
and also owned many slaves herself.

(C)

(12) Today the dungeons where they stayed are a museum. (13) Hundreds of people visit this museum each year to see where the slaves were held. (14) They view the dungeons and the House of the Slaves, which is where the masters lived. (15) Their is a memorial statue right outside the house showing African slaves in chains. (16) A visit there would is very educational. (17) You will learn a great deal from the guides about what happened there.

19. Sentence (1): Europeans played a large part in bringing slaves to America from west africa.

Which correction should be made to sentence 1?

a. replace played with were playing

b. insert a comma after America

c. insert a period after large part

d. change west africa to West Africa

20. Sentences (2) and (3): Because European countries sent out explorers who sailed down the west coast of Africa. They came in contact with the people there.

The most effective combination of sentences (2) and (3) would include which group of words?

a. coast of Africa while they

b. coast of Africa where they

c. coast of Africa instead of

d. coast of Africa but they

21. Sentence (4): They traded with them, but they also captures many of the people.

Which is the best way to write the underlined portion of this sentence?

a. had been captured

b. was capturing

c. will capture

d. captured

22. Which revision would improve the effectiveness of paragraph (B)?

a. move sentence (7) to the end of the paragraph

b. remove sentence (8)

c. remove sentence (9)

d. move sentence (11) to the beginning of the paragraph

23. Sentence (11): A group of free African women, called *signares*, sold food to the European traders for the enslaved people and also owned many slaves herself.

Which correction should be made to sentence (11)?

a. change owned to owns

b. change A group to A groups

c. insert a comma after people

d. replace herself with themselves

24. Sentence (15): Their is a memorial statue right outside the house showing African slaves in chains.

Which correction should be made to sentence 15?

a. move right to the end of the sentence

b. replace Their with There

c. change is to are

d. change slaves to Slaves

25. Sentence (17): You will learn a great deal from the guides about what happened there.

The most effective revision of sentence (17) would begin with which group of words?

a. If you go, you

b. Even if you go, you

c. However, you

d. Learning a lot

Questions 26 through 31 refer to the following employee memo.

What Will the New Procedures Do?

Memo
To: Employees of IMPEL
From: Management
Re: New Security Procedures
(5) Date: June 15
As a result of some incidents that have occurred with unauthorized persons in secure parts of Building A, as of June 30, new procedures will go into effect for security in
(10) that building. From now on, all employees reporting to work should enter through the employee entrance at the side of the building on Murray Street. No employee is to enter through the main entrance. In order to be
(15) admitted, each employee must have a valid photo ID. The ID needs to be swiped to unlock the door. Make sure not to allow another person to enter with you even if you know the person. Each employee needs to
(20) swipe his or her own ID in order to be registered as being on the job.

The main entrance will be for visitors only. The receptionist there will call the party that the visitor is coming to meet so that he
(25) or she can come to the main desk to escort the guest to his or her office. Visitors will be given temporary passes, but they cannot have full run of the office.

In addition, all employees will also be
(30) required to log in on their computer when they begin work and log out when they take a break. Make sure to log out and in when taking lunch breaks.

If an employee sees someone whom he
(35) or she believes is unauthorized to be in Building A, that employee should take immediate action and report the event to Mr. Shields, our head of security. Do not

approach the person, but simply call Mr.
(40) Shields's office. His extension is 890. If there is no answer, make a written report and e-mail it to cshields@impel.com.

If employees have any questions regarding these regulations, please contact
(45) the Human Resources department at extension 550. Ms. Hardy will be able to respond to your queries. Thank you for your cooperation in this matter. We feel that with these additional procedures, our workplace
(50) will be made more secure for everyone concerned. Ideally, this will result in improved work output, since any possibility of a security breach will be prevented.

26. Which of the following best restates the phrase "security breach" (line 53)?
   a. a compromise in the safety of the office
   b. a blow to the confidence of employees
   c. a distraction because of an employee's personal problems
   d. a defense against employees not doing their jobs

27. Based on the excerpt, which of the following can be inferred about management?
   a. They are concerned about the safety of employees.
   b. They believe that the office is completely secure.
   c. They want employees to fill out time sheets.
   d. They want to track employee work habits.

28. Which of the following could be prevented by the new security procedures?
   a. visitors entering through the main entrance
   b. employees swiping IDs to open doors
   c. employees entering through the side entrance
   d. unauthorized persons wandering around Building A

29. Imagine an employee sees a person in Building A without an ID badge. According to the memo, which of these actions should the employee take?
   a. call Mr. Shields's office to make a report
   b. tell the person to leave the building
   c. call the receptionist in the main entrance
   d. report the event to Ms. Hardy

30. Which of the following best describes the style in which this memo is written?
   a. complicated and unclear
   b. academic and dry
   c. straightforward and direct
   d. detailed and technical

31. Which of the following best describes the way in which the memo is organized?
   a. by listing information in the order of importance
   b. by sequence of events
   c. by presenting a problem and then a solution
   d. by comparing and contrasting issues

Questions 32 through 37 refer to the following excerpt from a novel.

Will His Mother Let Him Leave?

"Beatrice," he said suddenly, "I want to go away to school. Everybody in Minneapolis is going to go away to school."

Beatrice showed some alarm.

(5)   "But you're only fifteen."

"Yes, but everybody goes away to school at fifteen, and I *want* to, Beatrice."

On Beatrice's suggestion, the subject was dropped for the rest of the walk, but a

(10) week later she delighted him by saying, "Amory, I have decided to let you have your way. If you still want to, you can go away to school."

"Yes?"

(15)   "To St. Regis's in Connecticut."

Amory said nothing, but he felt a bolt of excitement along his spine.

"It's being arranged," continued Beatrice. "It's better that you should go away.

(20) I'd have preferred you to have gone to Eton and then to Christ Church, Oxford. But it seems impracticable now—and for the present, we'll let the university question take care of itself."

(25)   "What are you going to do, Beatrice?"

"Heaven knows. It seems my fate to spend my years in this country. Not for a second do I regret being American—indeed, I think that regret is very typical of ignorant

(30) people. I feel sure we are the great coming nation, yet"—and she sighed, "I feel my life should have slipped away close to an older, mellower civilization, a land of greens and autumnal browns. . . ."

(35)   Amory did not answer, so his mother continued, "My regret is that you haven't been abroad. But still, as you are a man, it's better that you should grow up here under the snarling eagle—is that the right term?"

(40)   Amory agreed that it was.

"When do I go to school?"

"Next month. You'll have to start East a little early to take your examinations. After that you'll have a free week, so I want you to

(45) go up the Hudson and pay a visit."

"To who?"

"To Monsignor Darcy, Amory. He wants to see you. He went to Harrow and then to Yale—became a Catholic. I want him

(50) to talk to you. I feel he can be such a help." She stroked his auburn hair gently. "Dear Amory, dear Amory. . . ."

Adapted from F. Scott Fitzgerald,
This Side of Paradise

32. Which of the following best expresses the main idea of the excerpt?

  a. A boy's mother agrees to let her son go to a boarding school.

  b. A boy's mother would like her son to visit schools in other countries.

  c. A boy wants to make his mother happy.

  d. A boy wants to get away from his hometown.

33. Based on the information in this excerpt, which of the following would Beatrice most likely prefer to do?

  a. learn about American history

  b. have a potluck dinner with friends

  c. spend time in England

  d. teach English to schoolchildren

34. Why does Beatrice most likely think it is better for Amory to grow up in America?

  a. He would not like Europe.

  b. He is good at sports.

  c. Schools are easier in America.

  d. He was born in America.

35. Based on Beatrice saying "I feel my life should have slipped away close to an older, mellower civilization, a land of greens and autumnal browns" (lines 31 to 34), what does she suggest about America?

  a. She thinks it is similar to England.

  b. She believes it is a land of great energy.

  c. She assumes it is a weak country with little future.

  d. She decides then to adopt it as her home.

36. How does Amory calling his mother by her first name influence the excerpt?

  a. It shows that Amory and his mother are not close.

  b. It shows that Beatrice wants to appear to be Amory's sister.

  c. It shows that Beatrice resents being a mother.

  d. It shows that Amory and his mother's relationship is not typical.

37. Why does Beatrice want Amory to visit Monsignor Darcy?

  a. She thinks that Monsignor Darcy can convince Amory to go to school closer to home.

  b. Monsignor Darcy is Amory's uncle.

  c. She wants Amory to become Catholic.

  d. She feels that Monsignor Darcy can help Amory because he went to Harrow and Yale.

Questions 38 through 42 refer to the following excerpt from a review.

What Does the Reviewer Think of *Last Fight*?

Last Fight may be one of the biggest blockbusters of the summer, but it doesn't live up to the buzz around it. In this science fiction tale of epic proportions, viewers are

(5)   propelled forward to a future when Earth is populated by androids and humans. These survivors of an ancient civilization live in a sterile world covered by a plastic dome. The dome is for protection from aliens who

(10)   attack Earth on a regular basis. It also cuts down on such environmental problems as air pollution and global warming.

      The plot centers around a young man named Raal and his quest to forge a peace

(15)   between the humans and the aliens. His is a

difficult task, considering the aliens have no desire to stop trying to overcome Earth and its inhabitants. While Raal (George Armstrong) is a likeable character, he lacks the ability to
(20) change expression to any extent. As a result, his acting range is quite limited. He is something of a dreamer, and perhaps the message here is that there is no place for dreamers in the future, but I will not detail
(25) the plot or the ending. I don't want to spoil it for those people who may actually want to view the film. Still, let it be said that events do not go well for young Raal.

The high point of the movie for me
(30) was the performance by veteran actor Bruce Cameron as the sage Kel. He has shown over and over his ability to transform even the most mundane character into someone fascinating to watch. It may be worth seeing
(35) the film just for his performance.

Besides being far-fetched, the movie concentrates too much on special effects, including 3-D, but that of course may be a draw for many viewers. Its cost was also
(40) enormous. Not much that is green is in this film.

38. Which of the following is the main idea of the excerpt?
   a. The author is giving the reasons movies should not use special effects.
   b. The author is detailing the kind of acting that he prefers.
   c. The author is providing his impressions of a science fiction movie.
   d. The author is explaining why he enjoys science fiction movies.

39. Which of the following best expresses the reviewer's opinion of *Last Fight*?
   a. It was too expensive to make and is too long.
   b. It was enjoyable because there was some great acting in it.
   c. The reviewer hopes that most people will turn out for the movie.
   d. It has little depth and relies too much on special effects.

40. If it is known that the author of this review had written numerous science fiction scripts, none of which were ever made into a movie, how would this most likely affect the reading of this review?
   a. The experiences of the author give his or her opinion greater value.
   b. The author's knowledge of the genre may be questioned.
   c. Much of the negativity might be construed as sour grapes.
   d. The author's personal experiences have no influence on the review whatsoever.

41. Which of the following best describes the style in which this review is written?
   a. technical
   b. humorous
   c. academic
   d. ornate

42. According to the author, which word best describes *Last Fight*?
   a. provocative
   b. lighthearted
   c. solemn
   d. overblown

Questions 43 through 50 are based on the following passage.

How to Write a Cover Letter

(A)

(1) A cover letter that accompanies your résumé is of great importance, the cover letter gives the employer a general impression of you. (2) In fact, if the cover letter don't interest the potential employer, the employer may opt not to read through the résumé at all. (3) So make your cover letter effective by keeping it short and bring up points that will interest the reader.

(B)

(4) Before you start to write, make sure you have an updated résumé. (5) Then research the company so you can include information about itself that might relate to the position you are hoping to fill. (6) Research will also help you prepare for an interview. (7) When you are ready to write your letter make sure to include the name of the person the title, the correct company name, and address. (8) If you don't know the name of the person to who you are writing, use "Dear Sir/Madam."

(C)

(9) When you get to the body of the letter, use the first paragraph to say why you think you would be good for the position.
(10) Also include, why you would want to work for the company. (11) Use the next paragraph to tell about your experience and matching it to the job. (12) Let the employer know that you are enthusiastic about the prospect of working for the company.
(13) The last paragraph should be brief.

(14) Should include a strong statement that will make the employer want to interview you. (15) At the end of the letter, give your contact, information and conclude with either "sincerely yours" or "yours truly."

43. Sentence (1): A cover letter that accompanies your résumé is of great importance, the cover letter gives the employer a general impression of you.

Which correction should be made to sentence (1)?
   a. insert a comma after <u>résumé</u>
   b. remove the comma
   c. replace <u>gives</u> with <u>give</u>
   d. replace the comma with <u>because</u>

44. Sentence (2): In fact, if the cover <u>letter don't interest</u> the potential employer, the employer may opt not to read through the résumé at all.

Which is the best way to write the underlined portion of sentence (2)?
   a. letter did not interest
   b. letters don't interest
   c. letter haven't interest
   d. letter doesn't interest

45. Sentence (3): So make your cover letter effective by keeping it short and bring up points that will interest the reader.

Which correction should be made to sentence (3)?
   a. change <u>keeping</u> to <u>will keep</u>
   b. change <u>interest</u> to <u>interesting</u>
   c. change <u>it</u> to <u>its</u>
   d. change <u>bring</u> to <u>bringing</u>

46. Sentence (5): Then research the company so you can include information <u>about itself</u> that might relate to the position you are hoping to fill.

Which is the best way to write the underlined portion of sentence (5)?
a. about yourselves
b. about herself
c. about himself
d. about yourself

47. Sentence (7): When you are ready to write your letter make sure to include the name of the <u>person the title</u>, the correct company name, and address.

Which is the best way to write the underlined portion of sentence (7)?
a. person; the title
b. person, the title,
c. person. The title
d. person and the title

48. Sentence (8): If you don't know the name of the person <u>to who</u> you are writing, use "Dear Sir/Madam."

Which is the best way to write the underlined portion of sentence (8)?
a. to which
b. that
c. which
d. to whom

49. Sentence (11): Use the next paragraph to tell about your experience <u>and matching</u> it to the job.

Which is the best way to write the underlined portion of sentence (11)?
a. getting to have matched
b. and to have matched
c. and to match
d. yet to match

50. Sentence (14): Should include a strong statement that will make the employer want to interview you.

What correction should be made to sentence (14)?
a. insert <u>It</u> before <u>Should</u> and use lowercase <u>should</u>
b. change <u>will make</u> to <u>is making</u>
c. replaced <u>interview</u> with <u>interviewing</u>
d. change <u>employer want</u> to <u>employer. Want</u>

Read the following passages. Then, read the prompt and write an essay taking a stance. Use information from the passages to support your essay.

President Franklin Roosevelt's Message to Congress on Establishing Minimum Wages and Maximum Hours, May 24, 1937

"Today, you and I are pledged to take further steps to reduce the lag in the purchasing power of industrial workers and to strengthen and stabilize the markets for the farmers' products. The two go hand in hand. Each depends for its effectiveness upon the other. Both working simultaneously will open new outlets for productive capital. Our Nation so richly endowed with natural resources and with a capable and industrious population should be able to devise ways and means of insuring to all our able-bodied working men and women a fair day's pay for a fair day's work. A self-supporting and self-respecting democracy can plead no justification for the existence of child labor, no economic reason for chiseling workers' wages or stretching workers' hours.

Enlightened business is learning that competition ought not to cause bad social consequences which inevitably react upon the profits of business itself. All but the hopelessly reactionary will agree that to conserve our primary resources of man power, government must have some control over maximum hours, minimum wages, the evil of child labor and the exploitation of unorganized labor."

Letter to the Editor Regarding Minimum Wage Increase, January 3, 2014

Dear Editor:
I have seen many people speak out in support of raising the minimum wage in recent weeks, but I have yet to see anyone offer an informed

alternative view. The truth is, if we increase the minimum wage for all American workers, we will undoubtedly do irreparable harm to our economy. The more we keep government from intruding into the workplace, the better.

Raising the minimum wage means that employers have to come up with the extra money to pay their workers more. How will they do this? By firing workers to reduce costs, or by charging more for their goods and services. If they fire workers, then those workers will now be earning less than they did before... not exactly a great solution to raise the standard of living. If they raise the price of goods and services, then people will have to spend more on life essentials such as food and transportation. So the benefit of higher wages will be eaten up by the increased expenses faced by the average worker.

When I was growing up, I made twenty-five cents an hour washing cars. I used that money to put myself through college to get my engineering degree. I used that degree to get a job designing bridges for the state of Texas. I didn't sit there at the car wash complaining about how little I earned; I used that opportunity to better myself. I just wish more people these days were willing to do the same.

Sincerely,

Ralph Phillips

Prompt

These two passages present different arguments regarding the issue of minimum wage. In your response, analyze both positions to determine which one is best supported. Use relevant and specific evidence from the passages to support your response.

Answers

1. a. Although Gilbert may feel *respect* and *gratitude*, the word that best describes his feelings is **love**. It is clearly indicated in his actions. *Nervousness* is not supported by the excerpt, nor is *fear*.

2. c. This choice is clearly supported by what the excerpt says happened when their eyes met— "and all doubt was swept away in a certainty that everything would be wonderful." The other choices may enter into the scene between them, but they do not occur when their eyes met.

3. d. It is clear from the ending of the excerpt that this was the biggest and hardest change for Anne. That is why she felt a "tinge of sadness." The other choices are not supported.

4. b. There are hints in the excerpt that support this answer, such as Marilla looking "gray" when Anne was leaving and how Anne had filled the house with "light and life." The other choices are not supported by the text.

5. b. Based on the information in the excerpt, this is the correct answer. The text says that Gilbert had won her "after years of patient waiting." This supports choice **b**, not the other choices.

6. d. The author gives the readers clues about what all the other characters are thinking, but the reader does not learn anything about Mr. Allan.

7. b. The text says that not many birds sang in September but that one sang sweetly while Gilbert and Anne repeated their vows. It even "wound up with one more little, glad trill" after the ceremony was over, seeming to mirror the joy of the wedding service.

8. d. Choice **d** is correct because it capitalizes all the words that make up the proper name of the college. Choices **a**, **b**, and **c** are incorrect because they capitalize some, but not all, of the words in the proper name.

9. c. The best revision of this sentence reads, "I am studying all types of farming techniques, but prefer organic methods for growing vegetables." Therefore, choice **c** is the best response. Choices **a**, **b**, and **d** change the meaning of the sentence.

10. d. Choice **d** is the best answer. This contains all the relevant information that is needed. Choice **a** is very general, and it is unclear what permanent position is wanted by the letter writer. Choice **b** is grammatically incorrect because it lacks a subject for the verb *apply*. Choice **c** is awkward and unclear.

11. d. Choice **d** is the best response, since this information is not central to the main point of the letter, which is asking for an internship. Choice **a** doesn't make sense when it is moved. Choice **b** doesn't work since the information is not material to the topic. Choice **c** would mean removing an important sentence from the paragraph.

12. d. Choice **d** is correct because it removes an unnecessary comma from the sentence. Choice **a** is not correct because it would insert an unnecessary comma. Choices **b** and **c** are not correct because these contain the wrong forms of the verbs.

13. b. Choice **b** is the best response. This sentence replaces the repetitive *he has* with the pronoun *who*. Choice **a** is a run-on sentence so it is incorrect. Choice **c** does not combine the sentences, but simply puts an inappropriate comma between them. Choice **d** improperly joins the sentences with *and*.

14. c. Choice **c** is correct because this action happened once in the past and is not ongoing. Choice **a** is not correct because the verb is in the present tense, not the past tense, the way it should be. Choice **b** is the wrong answer because it creates a phrase and doesn't address the verb problem. Choice **d** uses an incorrect form of past tense.

15. c. This is the best answer. The audition will give him a chance to be discovered. The audition will not make him become famous or give him a chance to make a good living.

16. c. The excerpt says Gene got to the audition site at 9:00 A.M. and had been waiting more than three hours (line 20). That would make the time after noon.

17. c. This answer reflects what happens in the story. At first he was slow to start, but then he sang very well and passed the round of auditions.

18. d. This answer reflects the feelings that Gene was having about the audition. For instance, a person's heart often beats loudly—or seems to beat louder than usual—when a person is experiencing an important moment in life.

19. d. Choice **d** correctly capitalizes a proper noun. Choice **a** changes the verb into an incorrect tense. Choice **b** inserts a comma that is not needed, and choice **c** makes the second sentence a fragment.

20. b. Choice **b** is correct because it combines the ideas in both sentences with the relative pronoun *where*. Choice **a** uses a transition word that changes the meaning of the sentences. Choice **c** creates a confusing sentence, and choice **d** changes the meaning of the sentences.

21. d. Choice **d** is correct because the verb form fits the subject, and the tense is correct as well. Choice **a** is not correct because the tense and the verb in the first part of the sentence do not match the subject. Choices **b** and **c** are both incorrect because they pick incorrect tenses—one in the present and the other in the future.

22. b. Choice **b** is correct. This sentence has nothing to do with the main topic of the paragraph, which concerns the slaves being held in Gorée Island. Choice **a** is not correct because this is a topic sentence and clearly the opening of the paragraph. Choice **c** has important information about the slaves in it. Choice **d** wouldn't make logical sense.

23. d. Choice **d** is correct since the subject (*women*) is plural, not singular. Choice **a** is incorrect because this is the wrong verb tense for the sentence. Choice **b** is grammatically incorrect since *a* is singular and *groups* is plural. No comma is needed after *people*, so choice **c** is incorrect.

24. b. Choice **b** is correct because it replaces the homonym *their*, a possessive pronoun, with *there*, meaning *that place*. Choice **a** does not make sense. Choice **c** would result in a verb that does not agree with the subject. Choice **d** is incorrect because there is no reason to capitalize *slaves*.

25. a. Choice **a** is correct because this phrase links a visit to Gorée Island with learning from the guides. Choice **b** is incorrect because it changes the meaning of the sentence. Choice **c** uses an inappropriate transition. Choice **d** is wrong because it turns the sentence into a dependent clause.

26. a. This phrase means that the security was somehow broken, so choice **a** is correct. This can be seen in the very first section of the memo: "As a result of some incidents that have occurred with unauthorized persons in secure parts. . . ." The other choices are not suggested by these words. They have nothing to do with security being compromised.

27. a. The point of the memo is that there were some security incidents that needed to be addressed. Based on the memo, choice **b** is clearly not correct, and the others are not suggested by the memo, either.

28. d. If you read the memo carefully, you will see that this is the one option that the new regulations will help prevent. It is mentioned in the first paragraph.

29. a. Again, a close reading of the text will reveal that this is what an employee is to do first if a stranger is seen in Building A. This can be found in the third paragraph.

30. c. The memo is direct and to the point. It is not technical. It's quite clear and not at all academic.

31. c. The memo states a problem at the beginning and then describes the new regulations that will solve it—a way to keep unauthorized people out of secure parts of Building A.

32. a. This choice is clearly correct. It contains the main idea of the excerpt. The dialogue is about a boy wanting to go away to school and his mother finally agreeing to it.

33. c. It seems clear from the dialogue in the excerpt that Beatrice would prefer to be in England rather than do any of the other activities. She seems not to mind America, but she does long for her native country.

34. d. This is the most logical choice, although it is never actually stated in the excerpt. There is no mention of the father, although he may or may not live in America. The other choices are not supported by the passage, either.

35. b. This is the only choice suggested by the lines spoken by Beatrice. She is comparing England's mellow nature to America's energetic spirit.

36. d. This is the best and most all-encompassing answer. This mother and son do not seem like most mothers and sons. The way they relate and talk suggests an atypical relationship.

37. d. This is the most obvious reason that Beatrice wants Amory to meet Monsignor Darcy. She says he went to Harrow and Yale, and she wants Amory to talk to him.

38. c. This is what the review is mostly about. The reviewer does address the other answer choices, but they do not represent the main intent of the review.

39. d. Based on what the reviewer says about the movie, this is the best answer. He says the acting is bad. He does not mention the length of the film, either.

40. c. This is the most logical choice. People reading the review would take into consideration that the reviewer has never had any of his or her science fiction scripts made into a movie. This would definitely taint the review, as he or she might be overly critical.

41. b. The review is somewhat *humorous*, or at least that is its intention. Although the 3-D aspect of the film is mentioned, that's not really enough to call the review *technical*. A technical review would probably have discussed the 3-D aspect at more length. None of the other choices properly describes the writing style of the review.

42. d. This word best describes what the reviewer feels about the movie. Overall, the reviewer is not very impressed with the film, so a positive choice like **b** could be eliminated. None of the other choices accurately describes the author's opinion.

43. d. Choice **d** is correct because it adds an appropriate conjunction to join the two sentences. Choice **a** inserts an unnecessary comma, and by removing the existing comma you create a run-on sentence, so both choices **a** and **b** are incorrect. Choice **c** replaces the correct form of the verb with an incorrect form.

44. d. Choice **d** is correct because the singular verb *doesn't* agrees with the singular noun *letter*. Choice **a** is incorrect because this is the wrong verb tense for this sentence. Choice **b** is incorrect, not because of the verb, but because of the plural form of *letter*. The sentence is referring to one letter, not multiple ones. Choice **c** is incorrect because this is a plural form of the verb.

45. d. Choice **d** is correct because it uses a verb that is parallel to *keeping*. Choices **a** and **b** are incorrect because they use an incorrect form of the verb. Choice **c** is not correct because it changes the pronoun object into a possessive.

46. d. Choice **d** is correct because this pronoun refers back to the antecedent *you*. Choice **a** is incorrect because it refers to more than one *you*. Choices **b** and **c** are incorrect because they refer to either *she* or *he* as antecedents.

47. b. Choice **b** is correct because commas are used between lists of items. Choices **a** and **c** are incorrect because they create sentence fragments. Choice **d** is not correct because *title* is not the last item in the list of items.

48. d. Choice **d** is correct because the preposition *to* takes the objective form of the pronoun *who*. Choice **b** is incorrect because *that* refers to an animal or thing, but not a person. Also, *which* does not refer to a person, so choices **a** and **c** are incorrect.

49. c. Choice **c** is correct because it matches the preceding verb *to tell*. Choices **a** and **b** are incorrect because they do not match *to tell*. Choice **d** is incorrect because it creates a confusing sentence.

50. a. Choice **a** is correct because it adds a subject to properly complete the sentence. Choice **b** changes a correct verb form into an incorrect one, as does choice **c**. Choice **d** is incorrect because it turns the sentence into two fragments.

Extended Response

For this prompt, an extended response should include some discussion of how the two passages differ in viewpoint regarding the issue of minimum wage. Specifically, Roosevelt's message to Congress emphasizes the need for government to establish livable requirements for wages and working conditions, while the letter to the editor asserts that government should keep out of private enterprise as much as possible. A successful extended response should also analyze the arguments presented in each passage. For the Roosevelt passage, the arguments focus on an appeal to emotion and charitable cooperation among all Americans. For example, Roosevelt refers to the way a "self-respecting democracy" should run. The letter to the editor, on the other hand, relies largely on personal experience to support its argument. Mr. Phillips also offers a logical argument regarding the effects of a minimum wage increase that some could consider one-sided; following the logic of this argument, workers should be paid as little as possible to keep everyone employed and to keep the price of goods low. A keen reader might even note the potential conflict between the Mr. Phillips's assertion that government should stay out of the affairs of business, and the fact that he got a job working for the government.

3 ▶ ESSENTIAL READING SKILLS

CHAPTER SUMMARY
This chapter will help you build the foundation you need to understand the fiction and nonfiction passages found on the GED® Reasoning through Language Arts test. You will learn to identify word parts, prefixes, suffixes, context clues, multiple word meanings, the author's point of view and purpose, and theme. It will also teach you to make predictions and synthesize what you read.

The key to doing well on the GED® Reasoning through Language Arts test is being able to comprehend what you read. Some questions will require you to simply recall facts and information that you have read. However, a number of questions require a much deeper understanding of the text.

Fiction passages make up one-fourth of the GED® Reasoning through Language Arts test. Nonfiction passages make up the remaining three-fourths. In this chapter, you will review comprehension skills needed to understand these passages. Keep in mind that the skills reviewed in this chapter are also important in comprehending literature in general.

Word Parts

To understand what a passage is about, you have to be able to determine the meanings of its words. Words are formed from a combination of root words, prefixes, and suffixes. **Root words** are the foundation of words.

Prefixes are added to the beginning of words to change their meanings. **Suffixes** are added to the ends of words to change their meanings.

Look at the following example:

unexpected = un + expect + ed

In the word *unexpected*, *un-* is the prefix, *expect* is the root word, and *-ed* is the suffix. Each of these parts works together to give the word meaning. Think about the differences in the meanings of the following sentences:

> *We expect her to call by 1:00 today.*
> *We expected her to call by noon yesterday.*
> *The fact that she did not call was unexpected.*

Adding the suffix *-ed* to the end of the word changes it to past tense. Adding the prefix *un-* to the beginning tells that the event was *not* expected.

> *Mario is an honest man.*

Let's look at the underlined word, *honest*. We know that honest means "truthful" or "trustworthy." So, the sentence lets us know that Mario can be trusted.

> *Mario is a dishonest man.*

In this sentence, the prefix *dis-* has been added to the root word *honest*. This prefix means "not," so we know that *dishonest* means "not honest." Adding the prefix has changed the meaning of the sentence. Now we know that Mario cannot be trusted.

> *Emily handled the package with care.*
> *Emily was careless with the package.*

The first sentence tells that Emily was gentle with the package. However, when the suffix *-less* is added to the root word *care*, the meaning changes. This suffix means "without," so *careless* means "without care."

> *Emily was careful with the package.*

This sentence uses the same root, *care*, but adds the suffix *-ful*. This suffix means "full of," so Emily was full of care when she handled the package.

Following are lists of some common prefixes and suffixes and their meanings. Knowing the meanings of these word parts can help you figure out meanings of words and help you better understand what you read.

Prefixes

- *co-*: with
- *de-*: to take away
- *dis-*: lack of, opposite of
- *ex-*: out of, previous
- *extra-*: outside, beyond
- *il-, in-, im-, ir-*: not
- *inter-*: between, among
- *mis-*: wrongly, badly
- *non-*: without, not
- *pre-*: before
- *post-*: after
- *re-*: again
- *sub-*: lower, nearly, under
- *super-*: above, over
- *trans-*: across
- *un-*: not

Suffixes

- *-able, -ible*: able to, can be done
- *-ant*: one who
- *-en*: made of
- *-er*: comparative, one who
- *-ful*: full of
- *-ive*: likely to
- *-ize*: to make
- *-less*: without
- *-ly*: in a certain way
- *-ment*: action, process
- *-ness, -ity*: state of
- *-or*: one who
- *-ous*: full of
- *-tion*: act, process

Now, use what you know about word parts to determine the meaning of the underlined word in the following sentence. Write the meaning of the word on the line underneath.

> *It seemed illogical for her to drop out of the campaign.*

_____

Breaking the underlined word into word parts can help determine its meaning. The word *illogical* is made up of the prefix *il-*, meaning "not," and the word *logical*. If something is logical, it makes sense. So, if it is illogical, it does not make sense.

> ### TIP
>
> Keep in mind that groups of letters are only considered a prefix or suffix if they are added to a root word. For example, *mis-* is a prefix when added to the root word *spell* to create the word *misspell*. However, these letters are not a prefix in the words *mistletoe* or *misty*.

Sometimes, thinking of a word with a similar root can help you figure out the meaning of an unfamiliar word.

> *The captain watched the sails <u>deflate</u> as he attempted to guide the boat to the dock.*

Suppose you do not know the meaning of *deflate*. Ask yourself, "Do I know a word that has a similar root?" You probably already know that *inflate* means to fill something with air or to make something larger.

> *Dad will <u>inflate</u> the balloons before the party.*

Using what you know about the meanings of word parts, you can figure out that *deflate* means that the air has gone out of something, or it has gotten smaller.

Let's try another example:

> *Brian carries his <u>portable</u> CD player everywhere he goes.*

Portable contains the root *port* and the suffix *-able*. Port means "to move," so *portable* means that the CD player is "able to be moved."

> *The company plans to <u>export</u> 75% of its products overseas.*

Suppose you are unsure of the meaning of *export*. Do you know a word that has a similar root? *Portable* and *export* have the same root. You know that the prefix in *export*, *ex-*, means "out of" and *port* means "to move," so *export* means "to move out." So, the company plans to move its products out and send them overseas.

> *The island <u>imports</u> most of its fruit from other countries.*

If *export* means "to move out," what do you think *import* means? It means "to move in" or "to bring in."

Now you try. What words could help you determine the meaning of the underlined word in the following sentence? Write the words on the line underneath.

> *She tried to <u>visualize</u> the author's description of the animal.*

_____

Vision and *visible* both have roots that are similar to that of *visualize*. *Vision* is the sense of sight. If something is *visible*, it is able to be seen. So, to *visualize* means "to see something."

Here are a few sets of words with similar roots. Knowing sets of words with similar roots can help you determine word meanings. What other words could you add to each set in the list below? What other groups of words can you think of that have similar roots?

- adjoin, conjunction, juncture
- anniversary, annual, biannual

- audible, audience, audio
- benevolent, benefit, beneficial
- chronic, chronological, synchronize
- civic, civilian, civilization
- contradict, dictate, dictionary
- describe, prescribe, transcribe
- design, signal, signature
- empathy, pathetic, sympathy
- evacuate, vacancy, vacuum
- exclaim, exclamation, proclaim
- mystify, mystery, mysterious
- pollutant, pollute, pollution
- telescope, telephone, television
- terrain, terrestrial, territory

Context Clues

Even great readers will come across unfamiliar words in a text at times. One way to figure out the meanings of these words is to use **context clues**. These are hints that are included in the sentence or passage that help readers understand the meanings of words.

Authors often use **synonyms**, or words with similar meanings, to help readers understand unfamiliar terms.

> Beginning this semester, students will have an _abbreviated_, or shortened, day every Wednesday.

In this sentence, the author included the synonym _shortened_ to explain what he or she means by _abbreviated_. This context clue helps readers determine the meaning of a word that might be unfamiliar.

An author might also include **antonyms**, or words with opposite meanings, to clarify the definition of a word.

> Please be advised that both _residents_ and visitors are expected to park their cars on the west side of the apartment building.

This sentence talks about _residents_ and _visitors_. So, we can conclude that residents are different than visitors. Because you probably know that visitors are people who do not live in the building, we can figure out that _residents_ are people who do live there.

Definitions or **explanations** are often used as context clues.

> The _reluctant_ child was not eager to share his project with the class.

In this sentence, the author explained the meaning of _reluctant_ by saying that the child was _not eager_.

Examples are another type of context clue that can be used to determine the meaning of unknown words.

> Ms. Greene pointed out pictures of several _monuments_ in the students' history books, including the Statue of Liberty, the Lincoln Memorial, and the Liberty Bell.

This sentence includes three examples of monuments: the Statue of Liberty, the Lincoln Memorial, and the Liberty Bell. From these examples, we can figure out that a _monument_ must be a famous place or structure that has a special importance.

TIP

When looking for context clues, be sure to check sentences surrounding the unfamiliar word. These clues might be contained in the sentences before or after the sentence that includes the word in question, or they may even be in another part of the paragraph.

As you read the following sentences, look for context clues that could help you determine the meanings of the underlined words. Then, answer the questions that follow.

> *We climbed all day before reaching the <u>apex</u>, or top, of the mountain. We hadn't eaten anything in several hours and were all <u>famished</u>. I was so extremely hungry that I couldn't wait for lunch. As we ate our picnic, we talked about many topics, some <u>frivolous</u>, others serious. After an hour of eating, relaxing, and enjoying the gorgeous view, we began our hike back down the trail.*

1. What is the meaning of *apex*?

_____

2. What clues helped you determine the meaning?

_____

The synonym *top* probably helped you figure out that *apex* means the top, or the highest point, of the mountain.

3. What is the meaning of *famished*?

_____

4. What clues helped you determine the meaning?

_____

The sentence explains that the hikers hadn't eaten anything in several hours. The following sentence includes the definition "extremely hungry." These context clues probably helped you figure out that *famished* means "extremely hungry" or "starving." Notice that some of the clues were in the sentence following the underlined word. Also, notice that clues were found in more than one place. Be sure to look throughout the entire paragraph for clues that can help you determine meaning.

5. What is the meaning of *frivolous*?

_____

6. What clues helped you determine the meaning?

_____

The paragraph states that some of the topics the hikers discussed were *frivolous* and others were *serious*. This use of an antonym tells us that something that is *frivolous* is not serious.

Multiple Meaning Words

Many words have more than one meaning. As we read, it is important to know which meaning the author intends to use. Consider the use of the word *stoop* in the following sentences:

> *Li sat on the front <u>stoop</u>, waiting for her neighbor to come home.*

> *David had to <u>stoop</u> to fit into the tiny door of his little brother's clubhouse.*

> *The other candidate is constantly telling lies, but I would never <u>stoop</u> so low.*

In the first sentence, *stoop* means "a small porch." In the second sentence, *stoop* means "to bend forward." In the third sentence, *stoop* means "to do something unethical."

So, if words have more than one meaning, how are you supposed to figure out which is correct? You'll have to use context clues. Think about which definition makes sense in that particular sentence.

Read the following sentence.

> *The detective said the intruders left without a <u>trace</u>.*

Which is the meaning of *trace* in this sentence?

    a. a tiny amount
    b. a remaining sign
    c. a type of drawing
    d. to find something

In the sentence, the detective could not find any remaining sign that the intruders had been there. Although each of the answer choices is a definition of *trace*, only choice **b** makes sense in the context of the sentence.

Author's Purpose

To fully understand what we read, we need to be able to figure out why the passage was written. An author always has a reason, or purpose, for writing. The **author's purpose** for writing a passage is usually one of the following:

- to entertain
- to inform
- to persuade

Understanding the author's reason for writing can help you better understand what you read. Different types of texts usually have different purposes. Many stories, plays, magazine articles, poems, novels, and comic strips are written to **entertain.** They may be fiction or nonfiction and may include facts, opinions, or both, but the purpose for writing them is to tell a story. These are intended to entertain readers and are meant for pleasure reading.

> *This summer while vacationing in Florida, I went parasailing with my mom. It was the most thrilling adventure I'd ever had! We floated from a giant parachute, hundreds of feet above the water, and soared over the beaches.*

This passage was written to entertain. It was intended to tell a story about the author's adventure. It does not try to teach any information, nor does it try to convince you to share an opinion about the topic.

Textbooks, encyclopedias, and many newspaper articles are written to **inform**. Their purpose is to give the reader information or to teach about a subject. Such passages will usually contain mostly facts and may include charts, diagrams, or drawings to help explain the information.

> *Parasailing is a sport in which a rider is attached to a large parachute, or parasail. The parasail is attached to a vehicle, usually a boat, by a long tow rope. As the boat moves, the parasail and rider rise up into the air.*

This paragraph teaches readers about the sport of parasailing. It contains facts and information about the topic. Readers may enjoy reading about the subject, but the author's reason for writing the passage was to inform.

Other material, such as commercials, advertisements, letters to the editor, and political speeches, are written to **persuade** readers to share a belief, agree with an opinion, or support an idea. Such writing may include some facts or statements from experts, but it will most likely include the author's opinions about the topic.

> *One of the most dangerous sports today is parasailing. Each year, many people are seriously injured, or even killed, while participating in this activity. Laws should be passed that prohibit such reckless entertainment. If people want to fly, they should get on an airplane.*

The author of this paragraph wants to convince readers that parasailing is a dangerous sport. The text not only includes opinions, but also facts that support the author's stand on the subject. Notice that strong words and phrases, such as *seriously injured*, *should*, and *reckless*, are included to stir up emotions in the readers. The author's purpose for writing this passage was to persuade readers to agree with his or her beliefs about parasailing.

BOOST

Did you know that the GED® test was originally created for military personnel and veterans who did not finish high school? That was in 1942. Five years later, New York became the first state to make the test available to civilians. By 1974, the GED® test was available in all 50 U.S. states.

Let's practice what you've learned about recognizing the author's purpose. Read the paragraph and determine whether it was written to entertain, inform, or persuade.

It was a quiet summer evening. The moon was full, and the sky seemed to hold a million stars. Outside, only the sounds of the crickets could be heard.

What was the author's purpose for writing this passage?

Did you recognize that the author's purpose was to entertain? The text did not try to teach anything or convince you to hold a certain opinion. It was simply written for the reader to enjoy.

Point of View

It is important to think about who is telling the story. This narrator may be someone who is a part of the story, or it may be someone outside of the events. The **point of view** refers to who is telling the story, which makes a difference in how much information the reader is given.

Some stories use a **first-person** point of view. In this case, one of the characters is telling the story, and readers see the events through this person's eyes.

After the game, Henry and I grabbed a pizza with the rest of the team. We hung out for a couple of hours, then headed home. By then, I was totally exhausted.

Notice that when an author uses a first-person point of view, the narrator uses the pronouns *I*, *me*, *us*, and *we*, and it seems as if the character is speaking directly to the reader. The narrator only knows his or her own thoughts and feelings, not those of the other characters, and often shares his or her attitudes and opinions with the readers.

Other stories use a **third-person** point of view, in which the narrator is not a character in the story and does not participate in the events.

After the game, Deon said he would join Henry and the rest of the team for pizza. They stayed for a couple of hours before heading home, exhausted.

When a story is told from the third-person point of view, the narrator will use pronouns such as *he*, *she*, and *they* when discussing the characters. Also, the narrator often knows the thoughts and feelings of every character.

Let's practice what you've just reviewed. Read the next three paragraphs, think about who is telling the story, and determine the point of view of the passage.

As soon as the bell rang, a tall, thin woman with dark hair rose from behind the desk. The class quieted as she began to speak.

"Good morning, class," she stated. "I am Ms. Wolfe, and I will be your English teacher this semester. Go ahead and open your books to the table of contents, and let's get started."

Ms. Wolfe picked up the text from her desk, and opened it to the first page.

What is the point of view of this passage?

_____

This passage is written in the third-person point of view. The narrator is not a character in the story. Notice that the pronoun *I* is included in the passage. However, it is spoken by one of the characters, not the narrator.

Theme

As we read, we look for and try to understand the messages and information that the author wants to share. Sometimes, the author's message is very obvious. Other times, we have to look a little harder to find it. The **theme** of a story is its underlying message. In a fable, the moral of the story is the theme. In fiction, this overall message is usually implied, rather than being directly stated, and may involve the following:

- attitudes
- beliefs
- opinions
- perceptions

The theme often leaves you with ideas, a conclusion, or a lesson that the writer wants you to take away from the story. Often, this lesson relates to life, society, or human nature. As you read, think about what the author's message might be. Consider the characters' words and actions, the tone, the plot, and any repeated patterns to see what views of the writer these portray.

Think about the story of the three little pigs. One could say that the theme of this story is that it is best to do a job the right way the first time. The author does not directly state this message, but this is a lesson or opinion that readers might take away from the story.

Common themes you may have found in reading might include:

- Crime does not pay.
- It is important to be honest.
- Be happy with what you have.
- Money cannot buy happiness.
- Keep going when things get tough.
- Do not be afraid to try something new.

Give it a try. Look for the theme as you read the following passage.

Camilla usually looked forward to Friday nights, but this week was the definite exception. Instead of going to the movies with her friends, she would be stuck at home, helping Mom get ready for tomorrow's garage sale. As she walked into the house, Camilla could see that Mom was already prepared for the long night ahead of them.

"Hey, get that scowl off your face and throw on your overalls," Mom called out cheerfully. "It won't be that bad."

Camilla changed clothes and headed to the garage, dragging her feet the whole way. Mom was elbow deep in an old cardboard box. She pulled out a raggedy, old stuffed dog.

"Mr. Floppy!" Camilla cried, excited to see her old friend. "I haven't seen him in years!"

"Your very first soft friend," Mom reminisced. "I'm assuming you'll be keeping him? Or would you like a 25-cent price tag to stick on his ear?"

Camilla set the old dog aside. She would definitely keep him. She helped Mom empty the rest of the box, sticking price tags on other old toys and books. They continued through the boxes, stopping to look through old photo albums together, telling funny stories about some of the useless gifts they'd collected, laughing at the hand-me-down clothes that had arrived at their house over the years, and modeling the silliest of them.

After a few hours, Mom looked at her watch. "Wow! It's nearly 8:00 already. Should we order a pizza?"

Camilla couldn't believe how late it was. She looked at her mom—who was wearing dusty overalls, five strands of Aunt Edna's old beads, and Granny's wide-brimmed Sunday bonnet—and couldn't help but laugh out loud. This was the best Friday night she could remember.

What is the theme of the story?
- **a.** Memories are a special part of life.
- **b.** It is important to get rid of old items.
- **c.** Families should spend weekends together.
- **d.** Sometimes things turn out to be better than expected.

At the beginning of the story, Camilla did not want to spend the evening helping her mom. By the end, she was having a great time. Choice **d** is the theme of this story. Some of the other answer choices represent ideas that were presented in the story, but the underlying message that the author wanted to portray is that things can turn out to be more fun than we think they will be.

Synthesis

Suppose you were doing a research paper. You would select a topic, then to be sure you learned as much as possible, you would search a variety of texts to find information about that topic. After reading each of your sources, you would put together all the information you learned. This combination of information would provide a clear understanding of the subject.

As readers, there are times when we have to combine information to gain a complete understanding of the text. **Synthesis** means putting ideas from multiple sources together. Sometimes, readers synthesize information from different parts of a single text. Other times, they must put together information from more than one text.

Read the passage below.

Roger quietly walked to the shelf. He pulled his ball cap down on his head as he quickly looked at the items neatly lined up in front of him. Then, he grabbed a package of crackers, shoving it into his backpack as he hurried to the door, trying not to make any sound.

Think about what you know so far. Roger is being quiet; he grabs something off of a shelf and tries to quickly sneak out the door. What do you think is happening? Now, continue reading.

Roger's mom heard him opening the front door. She put the sleeping baby in her cradle, then hurried to see her son. "Honey, did you find something in the pantry to take for a snack?"

"Yeah, Mom," Roger replied. "I found the peanut butter crackers and grabbed a package. Those are my favorites. Thanks for getting them."

"Do you want me to drive you to baseball practice so you're not late?" Mom asked.

"No, I don't want you to wake Amy. I know she hasn't been sleeping much lately."

"You're a good big brother and a great son. Be careful."

Did this new information change your mind about what was happening? You may have thought Roger was being sneaky or doing something he should not have been doing. When you synthesize the new information, you gain a deeper understanding of the situation. Roger is being quiet so he doesn't wake up his sister, he's taking crackers that his mom bought for him off of a shelf in the pantry, and he's in a hurry to get to practice.

When you synthesize information, ask yourself:

- Why is this new information relevant?
- Why was the new information given?
- How does it relate to the first part of the passage?
- How does this help me gain a deeper understanding of what I've read?
- In what ways does the new information change my ideas about the passage?

Another common type of question found on the GED® Reasoning through Language Arts exam is an **extended synthesis** question. First, you will read a passage. Then, you will be given a question. An additional piece of information about the passage or the author will be given within the question itself. You will have to combine the new information with what you read in the text to gain a deeper understanding of the passage.

First, figure out how the new information relates to what you previously read. Then, try to determine how this information helps you understand the reading passage in a deeper or different way.

Let's try an example. Be sure to read the passage carefully so that you will be able to understand the question that follows.

The winter had been especially cold. A thick, snowy blanket had covered the landscape for what seemed like months. Each day, the stack of firewood beside the house grew visibly smaller and smaller. This concerned Ella terribly. She continued to hope that the snow would be gone before the firewood.

Ella turned away from the window and returned to her writing. Somehow, writing about summer made the house feel warmer. Feeling the sun's bright rays on her face, walking barefoot in the green grass, fishing with her family, swimming in the refreshing water—these were things Ella dreamed and wrote of during the long winter months.

Here's an extended synthesis question:

The author of the passage lived during the nineteenth century in the midwestern United States. Based on the information in the story, as well as knowing the information about the author, which of the following best explains Ella's concern over the firewood?

    a. Most nineteenth century homes had large fireplaces.

    b. There was not much firewood available during the 1800s.

    c. Winters in the midwestern United States are extremely cold.

    d. Before electricity, people depended on firewood for heat and cooking.

Keep in mind that to correctly answer this question, you need to combine the information in the passage with the new information given in the question. Several answer choices could make sense. For example, it is true that many nineteenth-century homes had fireplaces and that winters in parts of the United States can be very cold. However, these facts do not consider the pieces of information that you need to synthesize.

From reading the passage, you know that Ella needs firewood. After learning the time period during which she lived, you are able to see how important firewood was for her survival. During the nineteenth century, homes did not have electricity. People had to have firewood to warm their homes and cook their meals. Choice **d** best synthesizes the information from both sources.

Let's try another example. Read the passage carefully, then read the question. Determine how the information in the question is related to the passage.

> *As the real estate agent walked up to the home, she admired her own photo on the "For Sale" sign in the front yard. She was anxious to get this home sold. Once inside with the homeowners, she explained the next step in selling their house.*
>
> *"Your beautiful home has been on the market for several weeks now without any offers. We need to consider our options. The carpet is definitely a little bit worn in one bedroom, the bathroom wallpaper is a bit out of date, and the front yard could use some new flowers. These issues could be deterring potential buyers. I think it is time we lower the price of your home by at least 15%, if you want to get it sold."*

The real estate agent will qualify for a large bonus if she sells one more house within the next month. Which of the following best describes the agent's motives in the passage?

    a. Her first concern is selling the house quickly so she can get the bonus.

    b. Her profit depends on the house selling for the highest possible price.

    c. She knows it is best for the owners to get the best price for their home.

    d. Her clients' home is currently overpriced for the neighborhood.

Based on the information in the passage, we do not know whether the home is overpriced, so choice **d** is incorrect. Choices **b** and **c** may be true. However, these do not take into consideration the additional information provided within the question. This information lets us know that if the house sells quickly, the agent will receive a large bonus. When added to the information in the passage that states that she wants to lower the price of the house, we can figure out that her motivation for dropping the price is to sell the house quickly so that she can get the bonus. So, the correct answer is choice **a**.

TIP

Remember to carefully read the extended synthesis questions. Look for the additional information within the question and think about how this information relates to the passage. The information is there for a reason. You will be expected to use it as you consider your answer.

Make Connections

To better comprehend text, it is important for readers to **make connections** between what they are reading and what they already know. Not only does this help readers gain insight, but it also helps to make the material more personal and relevant. This gives readers a deeper understanding of what they read.

There are three main types of connections that great readers make:

1. text-to-self
2. text-to-text
3. text-to-world

The connections readers make are neither correct nor incorrect. The same text may remind different readers of very different things. Connections with texts are personal, and they will mean different things to different readers. The important thing is that readers connect with the text in a way that makes it meaningful and understandable to them.

Text-to-Self

Connections that readers make between the reading material and their own personal experiences are **text-to-self** connections. These make the reading more personal. Statements that could help you make such connections include the following:

- This reminds me of when I . . .
- If I were this character, I would . . .
- If this ever happened to me, I might . . .

Think about the story we read about Camilla and the garage sale. Perhaps it reminded you of a garage sale you had, of a time you came across sentimental items, or of a situation in which time flew by with your family. These would be text-to-self connections.

Text-to-Text

Text-to-text connections occur when readers are able to make connections between the reading material and a text that they have previously read. To make such connections, think about whether the text reminds you of any of the following:

- a different book by the same author
- a book with similar characters, settings, or plots
- a book that includes similar situations or events
- a book about a similar topic
- information you read in a textbook, newspaper, or magazine

Did Camilla's story remind you of another character who reconnected with his or her mom? Have you ever read an article about having a garage sale? Can you think of a book about discovering your family history? If so, these would be examples of text-to-text connections.

Text-to-World

Connections that readers make between the reading material and something that happens in the real world are **text-to-world** connections. To make this type of connection, think about whether the text reminds you of:

- information you read on the Internet
- something you saw on TV or heard on the radio
- events that are happening in the real world

If you connected Camilla's story to a television documentary on relationships between parents and teenagers or if it reminded you that there is a garage sale happening in your neighborhood this weekend, you made a text-to-world connection.

Quiz

Now you've had a chance to review some of the skills needed to comprehend reading passages.

Directions: Read the following passages and choose the *one best answer* to each question.

Questions 1 through 5 refer to the following passage.

What Will Happen with the Painting?

After hours of rummaging through the various items that had been donated to the charity over the weekend, Natasha was ready to head home for the day. She had sorted the
(5) clothing, books, toys, housewares, and sporting goods into the appropriate bins and would tackle the task of pricing the items in the morning. With any luck, the items would find their place on the store shelves by
(10) tomorrow afternoon and be sold quickly.

As she turned to lock the door to the storeroom, Natasha noticed a framed canvas leaning against the wall. She wondered where it had come from and why she hadn't
(15) noticed it before now. She bent over to examine the artwork and was amazed at the bold colors and brushstrokes of the oil painting and the detail in the carved wooden frame. At the bottom corner of the
(20) piece, she noticed the signature of a world-famous artist. Amazed, she stared at the painting wondering whether it was authentic or a fake. Natasha carefully traced the frame with her finger, looking for any imperfections.
(25) She couldn't help but wonder why someone would part with such a beautiful, and possibly valuable, piece of art. She carefully covered the painting with a sheet and placed it in a closet where it would be safe.

(30) Natasha could not stop thinking about the painting. Her mind was filled with questions that kept her awake most of the night. Where had it come from? Was it really the work of a famous artist? Why would
(35) someone give away a piece of art that could potentially be worth thousands of dollars? Finally, she got out of bed and went to the computer. She found the name of an art history professor at the nearby university.
(40) Maybe some of Natasha's questions would finally be answered.

1. Which is most likely the author's purpose for writing this passage?
   a. to tell readers a true story
   b. to inform readers about art history
   c. to entertain readers with a fiction tale
   d. to teach readers about a famous artist

2. Which is the meaning of the word *authentic* in line 22?
   a. old
   b. genuine
   c. famous
   d. beautiful

3. Read the following sentence from the second paragraph:
   Natasha carefully traced the frame with her finger, looking for any *imperfections*.

   What is the meaning of *imperfection*?
   a. perfect
   b. improvement
   c. type of disease
   d. a flaw or defect

4. Which statement is an example of a text-to-world connection readers might make with the passage?

   a. I remember when I found a high-fashion coat at a garage sale for only $5.

   b. Art appreciation has been on the rise in major cities.

   c. I need to clean out my attic and donate what I find to charity.

   d. An art history book I read mentioned that people sometimes don't realize they own valuable pieces of art.

5. Natasha spent many years working in an art museum and has a keen eye for valuable oil paintings. The charity she now volunteers with donates money to the local children's hospital, which is known for its impressive research program. Which sentence most accurately describes Natasha?

   a. She has a large art collection that she hopes to expand.

   b. She plans to return to the university and teach about art.

   c. She is generous and genuinely cares about helping others.

   d. She hopes to work in the field of medicine or research someday.

Questions 6 through 10 refer to the following passage.

Will Others Change Their Minds?

Since I was a boy, it has been difficult to make friends. Many assumed that all aristocrats thought themselves better than others, but that was not the case. I never
(5) believed that being a member of the highest social class made me more important than anyone.

In the streets, people stepped far out of my way, as if trying to avoid me. I smiled and
(10) tried to make eye contact, but no one would meet my gaze. Groups of friends gathered on street corners and in cafes, laughing together. Loneliness filled my heart, and I longed to be a part of one of their groups. Yet somehow, I
(15) would be excluded by circumstances that many would call fortunate.

One day, I stopped at the farmers' market in town to buy a piece of fruit. As I paid the gentleman, a woman sneered and
(20) said, "Don't you have servants to do your shopping for you?" Several other customers giggled and turned their backs. Smiling politely, I thanked the man for the fruit and walked away, listening to the whispers
(25) behind me.

As I walked away, I noticed a young boy sitting alone beside the bakery. He was crying, and many people walked past him without stopping. I sat down beside him on
(30) the ground and asked why he was upset.

"I can't find my mother. I stopped to look in the window of the bakery. When I turned back around, she was gone," the boy explained.
(35) I put my arm around him, explaining that he was wise to stay in one place so that his mother could find him. "You must feel lonely," I said. "I feel lonely, too, sometimes.

(40) We'll stay here together until your mother returns."

Very soon, a frantic young woman came running down the street, calling out, "William! William, where are you?"

The boy jumped up, and his mother
(45) ran to us and scooped up her son in her arms, asking if he had been afraid.

"No, Mama," William explained. "This man kept me company."

The woman looked at me and seemed
(50) surprised, then smiled warmly and thanked me. William gave me a hug, then walked away, hand in hand with his mother. As they walked away, I realized a crowd had gathered to watch the commotion. One person in the
(55) crowd smiled at me, then another, then another. For the first time, I no longer felt like a lonely outsider.

6. Which sentence from the passage reveals its point of view?
   a. I smiled and tried to make eye contact, but no one would meet my gaze.
   b. Groups of friends gathered on street corners and in cafes, laughing together.
   c. "Don't you have servants to do your shopping for you?"
   d. He was crying, and many people walked past him without stopping.

7. Considering the point of view from which the story is told, which of the following is true?
   a. The narrator is not one of the characters in the story.
   b. The narrator knows the motivations of all the characters in the story.
   c. Readers will only know the thoughts and feelings of one character.
   d. Readers will know the thoughts and feelings of all the characters.

8. Reread the first paragraph. Which would best describe someone who is an *aristocrat*?
   a. friendly
   b. gloomy
   c. helpful
   d. wealthy

9. Which statement is an example of a text-to-self connection that readers might make with the passage?
   a. It was hard for me to make friends after I moved to a new town, and for a while, I felt like an outsider.
   b. Farmers' markets are growing in popularity.
   c. There was a missing child on the news last night, but he was found this morning, safe and sound.
   d. Our social studies book talks about class conflict throughout history.

10. What is the theme of the story?
   a. Friendship is a necessary part of life.
   b. It is difficult to find happiness without having great wealth.
   c. Even young children are able to make a difference in the world.
   d. It is important not to judge people before getting to know them.

Answers

1. c. This passage was written to entertain. It is not a true story, and although art history and a famous artist are mentioned, the author did not intend to teach readers about these topics.

2. b. The passage tells us that Natasha wondered whether the painting was "authentic or a fake." *Fake* is given as an antonym of *authentic*. So, *authentic* means *real*, or *genuine*.

3. d. The root of *imperfections* is *perfect*. The prefix *im-* means "not," so *imperfections* cause something to be not perfect. An *imperfection* is a flaw or defect that makes something not perfect. If you thought the answer was *perfect*, you selected the root of the word. If you chose "a type of disease," you may have confused the word with *infection*.

4. b. Choices **a** and **c** are examples of text-to-self connections because they relate ideas from the passage to something personal. Choice **d** makes connections between the passage and other texts that have been read previously, so it is an example of a text-to-text connections. Choice **b**, making a connection between the passage and something happening in the world, is a text-to-world connection.

5. c. This is an example of an expanded synthesis question. To answer it correctly, you must combine the information given in the question with what you read in the passage. Because Natasha used to work in a museum and recognizes valuable oil paintings, she probably had a pretty good idea that the artwork was worth a lot of money. The charity that now has the painting donates its money to the children's hospital, which uses some of the money for research. Natasha was obviously excited about the painting being given to the charity, which is probably because the money it raises will be given to the hospital. If she is so excited, she must really care about the people who will benefit from the donation.

6. a. This passage was written from the first-person point of view. The narrator is one of the characters in the story, and he uses pronouns such as *I* and *me*. Notice that it sounds as if the narrator is talking directly to the reader.

7. c. Because the story tells a first-person account of the events, only the narrator's thoughts and feelings will be revealed to the readers. The narrator is a character in the story, and he only knows his own ideas and motivations, unless the other characters reveal their thoughts and feelings to him.

8. d. Context clues in the first paragraph explain that an *aristocrat* is "a member of the highest social class." Generally, people in this class have a lot of money. In this story, the aristocrat was also friendly, helpful, and possibly even gloomy. However, by definition, aristocrats are usually wealthy. As you read, remember to look for context clues in the sentences surrounding the word they help to define. In this case, the word *aristocrats* is used in one sentence, and the definition or explanation is in the sentence that follows.

9. a. Choices **b** and **c** are examples of text-to-world connections because they relate ideas from the passage to real-world events. Choice **d** makes connections between the passage and other texts that have been read previously, so they are examples of text-to-text connections. Choice **a**, making a connection between the passage and something personal, is a text-to-self connection.

10. d. In this passage, people made assumptions about the narrator without getting to know him. As it turned out, these assumptions were incorrect. After others saw his helpfulness and the way he cared for the little boy, they became aware of his true personality. The narrator longed for friendships and showed that he felt helping the little boy was important, but these ideas were not the overall message the author wanted to portray. Choice **b** is the opposite of what the narrator believed, as he did have great wealth but was not happy.

In this chapter, you have learned seven strategies to help you better comprehend reading materials:

1. Breaking unfamiliar words into word parts, such as prefixes, suffixes, and root words, can be helpful in determining a word's meaning. Thinking of words with similar roots can also help readers figure out the meaning of unknown words.

2. Context clues such as synonyms, antonyms, definitions, and examples can be helpful in figuring out the meanings of unknown words. These clues may be in the same sentence as the unfamiliar word or in the surrounding sentences and paragraph.

3. Point of view refers to who is telling the story. First-person point of view is when one of the characters tells the story and readers see the events through his or her eyes. Third-person point of view is when the story is told by a narrator who is outside of the story and does not participate in the events. However, he or she is often aware of the thoughts and feelings of all the characters.

4. Authors usually write for one of the following purposes: to entertain, to inform, or to persuade.

5. The theme of a story is the author's underlying message. Usually, these beliefs, attitudes, or perceptions are not directly stated; instead, the theme is a lesson that readers take away from the story. The words and actions of the characters, the tone, the plot, and repeated patterns in the story help to reveal the theme.

6. Synthesizing information means putting together information from multiple sources or from more than one location within a source. Combining information can help readers gain a deeper understanding of the text.

7. Making connections between the text and what they already know helps readers better understand the material. The types of connections readers make include text-to-self, text-to-text, and text-to-world.

ESSENTIAL GRAMMAR SKILLS

CHAPTER SUMMARY

This chapter covers GED® test writing tips and strategies that will help you be successful on exam day. You'll learn to recognize and correct errors in sentence structure, usage, mechanics, and organization, as well as identify the purpose of various parts of an essay.

As you've seen in previous chapters, the GED® Reasoning through Language Arts exam tests both reading and writing skills. Don't let that get you worried—the good news is that preparing for one part helps you to prepare for the other. And of course, the more you practice, the better your score will likely be.

GED® Test Strategies

In this chapter, we focus on basic grammar and writing skills. The topics covered include:

- sentence structure
- usage
- mechanics
- organization

In addition, we also go over some GED® test tips and strategies. Together with the information provided in previous chapters, these proven tools for exam success will help you prepare for and excel on test day.

Sentence Structure

Sentence structure basically refers to the order and use of words in sentences. The simple sentence *He eats a burger* is written with good structure; all the words are in order and the sentence makes sense. The sentence *A he burger eats* contains the same words, but does not display good structure.

Sentence structure questions on the GED® test will be a little more difficult than the previous example, but they will be based on the same idea: that there are rules in English which govern where words should be placed in a sentence and how they are used. It's important for you to know what these rules are.

Subjects and Predicates

The subject is who or what is doing the action in the sentence; the predicate is the verb and everything that comes after it. For example, consider the following sentence:

Only geeks like tests.

In this sentence, *geeks* is the subject and *like tests* is the predicate.

Independent/Dependent Clauses

A clause is a group of words that contains a subject and a predicate. For example, the phrase *when I go to lunch* is a clause because it contains a subject (*I*) and a predicate (*go to lunch*). The phrase *to lunch* contains no subject and no verb, so it is not a clause.

There are two different kinds of clauses: independent and dependent. An independent clause is a complete sentence, whereas a dependent clause cannot stand alone as a sentence.

The phrase *when I go to lunch* is a dependent clause because it does not express a complete thought. Whatever the rest of the thought is, it's definitely necessary to make *when I go to lunch* a complete sentence.

Because people often speak in incomplete sentences, it can be difficult to tell the difference between a dependent clause and an independent clause. Fortunately, there are a number of clue words that generally come at the beginning of a phrase and tip us off that it's a dependent clause. (The technical name for these clue words is subordinating conjunctions.)

Here are some examples of clue words, or subordinating conjunctions:

after	if	when
as if	since	where
although	so that	which
because	that	while
before	though	
even though	until	

Memorize a few of these clue words each day, and by the time you take the test you should be able to recognize a dependent clause pretty easily.

Fragments and Run-ons

A fragment is a part of a sentence, or an incomplete sentence. A run-on is two or more sentences stuck together without proper punctuation. On the GED® test, fragments will often be dependent clauses, as in the previous example, and you'll be able to recognize them using clue words. At other times they will simply be groups of words lacking either a subject or a predicate. Look for a subject and a predicate in each sentence. If you can't find one, it's a fragment.

On the GED® test, a run-on often shows up in the form of two independent clauses joined by a comma, instead of separated by a period. For example, you might see a sentence like this:

> She agreed to marry him, that made
> him happy.

There are two complete thoughts here: *she agreed to marry him*, and *that made him happy*. They should be two separate sentences, as follows:

> *She agreed to marry him. That made
> him happy.*

BE CAREFUL

Anytime you see two phrases joined by a comma in a GED® test question, check to see whether they should be separated into two complete sentences.

People commonly mistake a number of words for coordinating conjunctions, but they actually require a separate sentence. If you come across any of these words on a GED® test question, it's a good chance that you're looking at a run-on:

also	indeed	then
besides	instead	therefore
furthermore	meanwhile	thus
however	now	while

Active and Passive Voice

Active and passive voice refers to the way you write about the subject and verb. If the subject is known and is doing the action, it's an active voice. If the subject is unknown or is not doing the action, it's a passive voice.

This concept is much easier to understand with an example. Look at the following sentence:

> *Barry hit the ball.*

Barry is the subject and he's the one doing the action. That means the sentence is written in an active voice. What if we write the following:

> *The ball was hit by Barry.*

Now *the ball* is the subject, but it's not doing anything; something is being done to it. The subject is no longer active, so the sentence is written in a passive voice.

Generally speaking, you should use the active voice, rather than the passive voice, when you write. The GED® test will likely include some questions that test your ability to identify the passive voice and to change it to an active voice.

Usage

Throughout the history of the English language, people have developed conventional ways of speaking that enable them to understand each other. These conventions are referred to as usage. On the GED® test, usage questions commonly test the following concepts:

- verb conjugation
- verb tense
- subject-verb agreement

Verb Conjugation

To conjugate a verb means to change its form so that it matches its subject correctly. For example, if your subject is *the dinosaur* and the verb is *want*, you would change the verb to *wants* to make it match the subject in the sentence, as in *The dinosaur wants to eat fruit*.

Although it may seem pretty easy to catch the error in the sentence, *The dinosaur want to eat fruit,* sentences that test your knowledge of verb tenses on the GED® test can be a little trickier. They will often contain multiple verbs separated by other words, like this:

The children are hungry and, thanks to their mom, is about to have a snack.

The verb *is* is incorrectly conjugated; the subject, *children*, is plural, and therefore the verb should be plural, too. The verb *are* matches the plural subject. The corrected sentence is:

The children are hungry and, thanks to their mom, are about to have a snack.

Verb Tense

Verb tense refers to the time in which an action occurs: past, present, or future. Most verbs have a different form for each tense. For example, the verb *drink* looks different if you're referring to the past, *drank*, than if you're referring to the future, *will drink*.

The GED® test is mostly concerned with your ability to keep tenses consistent. In other words, if you start a sentence with a verb in past tense, you should probably continue to use the past tense throughout.

Subject-Verb Agreement

As previously mentioned, a subject and verb are said to *agree* when they are either both plural or both singular. Usually, to make a noun plural you add an *-s*, and to make a verb plural you take an *-s* away. For example:

The dog growls.

or

The dogs growl.

On the GED® test, you're likely to see questions that will test common errors in subject-verb agree-

ment. Here are a few common mistakes to watch out for:

- **doesn't/don't.** Incorrect: *He don't want to go.* Correct: *He doesn't want to go.*
- **wasn't/weren't.** Incorrect: *The pens wasn't in the drawer when I looked.* Correct: *The pens weren't in the drawer when I looked.*
- **there's/there are.** Incorrect: *There's a lot of people here.* Correct: *There are a lot of people here.*
- **here's/here are.** Incorrect: *Here's the instructions.* Correct: *Here are the instructions.*

Mechanics

In reference to writing, the term *mechanics* refers to the little things that make your writing look like it should: capitalization, spelling, and punctuation. Using correct mechanics may not change the substance of your writing; that is, a word may mean the same thing whether it's capitalized or not. Correct mechanics will change how your writing is perceived.

Capitalization

You probably remember that in English, all proper nouns are capitalized. But you may sometimes have trouble remembering what a proper noun is. The following list includes many common nouns that should always be capitalized.

- People's first, middle, and last names and initials: *Bob Jones, T. Davis, Jay Lynn Jackson*
- Names of specific places: *Austin, Mississippi, Afghanistan, Rohnert Park*
- Brand names: *Band-Aid, Starbucks, McDonald's*
- Days of the week and holidays: *Sunday, Monday, Thanksgiving, Memorial Day*
- Months of the year: *August, September, October*

- Titles of books, movies, TV shows, etc., with the exception of short prepositions or articles that are not the first word: *War and Peace, Desperate Housewives, Harry Potter and the Sorcerer's Stone*

PROPER NOUNS

With proper nouns, a good rule to remember is *proper = property*. If someone owns the name (like *Wal-Mart*, for example), it probably has to be capitalized.

Most nouns in English are not capitalized, so it would be next to impossible to write a list of all types of nouns that shouldn't be capitalized. There are, however, several types of nouns that are commonly capitalized by mistake. Here are a few to remember:

- Words that refer to people's titles (doctor, secretary, president), unless they immediately precede the person's name: *my doctor, Doctor Jones, Secretary of State Roberts, the president, President Obama*
- Names of general places: *our city, the next town, seven continents, a park*
- General product names: *bandage, coffee, fast food*
- Seasons of the year: *fall, winter, spring, summer*

The general rule here is that unless you're referring to a specific person, place, or thing, the noun should not be capitalized.

Spelling

Good spelling skills are a lifelong pursuit. There is no fixed set of rules that you can memorize in order to know how to spell every word in the English language. Fortunately, the GED® test tends to test the same words over and over again—short, common words that people misspell all the time. Here's a list of some you should definitely know how to use:

its/it's	buy/by
their/there/they're	every day/everyday
who's/whose	know/no
your/you're	may be/maybe
affect/effect	passed/past
all right/alright	right/rite/write
than/then	weather/whether
to/too/two	which/witch
weak/week	

Punctuation

Much more than spelling, punctuation in English tends to follow a fixed set of rules. The problem is that the list of rules is half a mile long. Fortunately, for the purposes of the GED® test you will only need to know what each punctuation mark means and a few basic rules for how it is used.

- A **comma** (,) indicates a brief pause. Example: *Jackie, my oldest sister, got a job yesterday.*
- A **semicolon** (;) is used to divide two complete sentences with a pause shorter than a period. Example: *Jackie is my oldest sister; I don't get along with her.*
- A **colon** (:) introduces a list or an explanation. Example: *I have three sisters: Jackie, Celia, and Amber.*
- A **dash** (—) is used to indicate a long break for emphasis. Example: *My oldest sister and I used to fight—a lot.*
- A **period** (.) stops a sentence at the end of a complete thought. Example: *Jackie is my oldest sister.*
- An **exclamation point** (!) stops a sentence with emphasis. Example: *I'm sick of fighting!*
- A **question mark** (?) is used to indicate a question. Example: *Do you fight with your sisters?*

Among all punctuation marks in the English language, the comma interests the GED® test developers most. They want to know that you can use a comma when it's needed and leave it out when it's not. The following is a list of common comma uses:

- when you're combining two complete sentences with a coordinating conjunction (*and*, *but*, *or*, etc.)

  Example: *I don't like grammar, but I have to learn it for the test.*

- when you're writing a list of three or more related words

  Example: *The president is focused on the economy, health care, and the war in Afghanistan.*

- when you're using a quotation

  Example: *Who originally said, "All that glitters is not gold"?*

- when you're giving the reader extra information that's unnecessary to the sentence

  Example: *Jackie, my oldest sister, got a job yesterday.*

- when you're writing a date

  Example: *Today is November 14, 2009.*

COMMAS

Believe it or not, entire books are written on how to use commas correctly. Check out *Eats, Shoots & Leaves: Why, Commas Really Do Make a Difference!*

Organization

Organization refers to placing sentences and paragraphs in order so that the reader can best understand what you're trying to say in your writing. An organized paragraph typically includes one topic sentence,

placed either at the beginning or at the end of the paragraph, and a few supporting sentences. An organized essay includes an introduction with a strong thesis statement, two or more body paragraphs, and a conclusion.

There are several common ways of organizing supporting sentences and paragraphs in an essay. Three of the most common are:

1. chronological order
2. order of importance
3. cause and effect

Chronological Order

Chronological order is the order in which things happen in time; in other words, what happens first, next, and last. If you were telling a story, giving instructions, or relating an event in your essay, you would probably do well to write in chronological order.

A common mistake made by beginning writers is to skip around in time. For example, when telling about a football game, one might write:

> *Our team got a touchdown! The running back got the ball at the 48 yard line and ran it all the way to the end zone. The coach told the quarterback to go long, but instead he handed it off to the running back.*

As you can see, this is not the order in which things actually happened; that is, it's not written in chronological order and may be confusing to some. A more organized way to write the paragraph would be as follows:

> *The coach told the quarterback to go long, but instead he handed it off to the running back at the 48 yard line. Then the running back ran the ball all the way to the end zone. At last our team got a touchdown!*

Telling what happens first, next, and last—in that order—helps the reader keep track of what you're writing about.

TRANSITION WORDS

Transition words help readers know the direction you're going in your writing. Common transition words for chronological order include: *first, to begin, next, then, afterward, last,* and *finally*.

Order of Importance

To organize your writing based on order of importance means to put sentences or paragraphs in order from most to least important, or from least to most important. For example, let's say you're telling a coworker about your rotten weekend. Three terrible things happened to you: you lost your hat, you stubbed your toe, and you were very ill. Assuming that your illness is the most important event and losing your hat is the second most important event, you might tell the story like this:

> *This was a terrible weekend. I stubbed my toe so badly that now I can hardly walk. Even worse, on Saturday night I lost my hat. Worst of all, when I came home Saturday night I got violently ill!*

On the GED® test, you'll be expected to know when sentences or paragraphs are in the wrong order. Look for key words like *more/most, worse/worst* and *better/best* to determine what order things should be in.

Cause and Effect

Cause and effect is an organizational style that either puts the entire cause of an event first, and then the effect, or vice versa. The key to this method is to be sure that the two are entirely separated and clear. For example, let's say you got in a car wreck because a deer ran out in front of you. You might write something like this:

> *(1) Last week, I had to get my front bumper replaced. (2) I also had to get my windshield replaced and the front tires realigned. (3) All this trouble came into my life because I ran into a deer last Monday.*

As you can see, the two sentences describing the effect are together at the beginning of the paragraph, while the sentence describing the cause is at the end. The paragraph would not be as well organized if you moved sentence (3) in front of sentence (2), thereby interrupting the organizational flow.

Quiz

Now that you've had a chance to review the writing skills needed to do well on the GED® test, give the following questions a try. Read each question, and then choose the one best answer for each.

1. Sentence (1): Every time my brother takes a shower, he leave a huge mess.

   Which revision should be made to sentence (1)?
   a. replace *Every* with *All*
   b. change *takes* to *take*
   c. change *leave* to *leaves*
   d. replace *mess* with *messy*

2. (1) I used to enjoy going out to dance. (2) When I was younger.

   Which revision should be made to sentence (2)?
   a. delete sentence (2) and add a sentence about dancing
   b. move sentence (2) in front of sentence (1) and add the word *However*
   c. add *for example* to the beginning of sentence (2) and *instead of* at the end of sentence (1)
   d. connect the sentences by removing the period at the end of sentence (1) and set *When* in lowercase

3. (1) She ate the cake. (2) Which the king had poisoned.

   Which revision should be made to sentence (2)?
   a. delete the word *which*
   b. change the word *Which* to *That*
   c. connect sentences with a comma instead of a period and set *Which* in lowercase
   d. add the word *And* to the beginning of the sentence

4. Sentence (1): Three of us began the race, however, only two of us finished it.

   Which revision should be made to sentence (1)?
   a. move *Three of us began the race* to the end of the sentence
   b. change the first comma to a period and capitalize *however*
   c. delete *however* and replace with *because*
   d. change *however* to *nevertheless*

5. Sentence (1): The car was smashed by a cement mixer.

   Which revision should be made to sentence (1)?
   a. delete *was*
   b. place a period after *smashed*
   c. move *cement mixer* in front of *car*
   d. change the order to *A cement mixer smashed the car*

6. Sentence (1): The last time I went to see my friend in Dallas, he's living on the south side.

   Which of the following revisions should be made to sentence (1)?
   a. delete *The*
   b. change the comma to a period and capitalize *he's*
   c. change *he's* to *he was*
   d. move *he's living on the south side* to the beginning of the sentence

7. Read the sentences and then choose the best answer.

(1) Last week I had too get my front bumper replaced. (2) I also has to get my windshield replaced and the front tires realigned. (3) All this trouble came into my life, because I ran into a deer last Monday.

Which of the following revisions should be made to sentence (1)?

a. move *Last week* to the end of the sentence
b. change *too* to *to*
c. delete the word *front*
d. change *has* to *had*

8. Sentence (2): I also has to get my windshield replaced and the front tires realigned.

Which of the following revisions should be made to sentence (2)?

a. delete *also*
b. change *has* to *had*
c. add a comma after *replaced*
d. add a semicolon after *and*

9. Sentence (3): All this trouble came into my life, because I ran into a deer last Monday.

Which of the following revisions should be made to sentence (3)?

a. delete the comma after *life*
b. move *because I ran into a deer last Monday* to the beginning of the sentence
c. add a comma after *deer*
d. change *Monday* to *monday*

10. Which of the following should a good introduction do?

a. summarize the essay
b. develop the argument
c. get the reader's attention
d. leave the reader with a sense of closure

Answers

1. c. The subject and verb must agree. The singular subject, *he*, requires a singular verb.

2. d. By itself, sentence (2) is a fragment. Connecting it to sentence (1) makes it a dependent clause of a complete sentence.

3. c. By itself, sentence (2) is a fragment. Connecting it to sentence (1) makes it part of a complete sentence.

4. b. When the word *however* is used between two clauses, you can either place a period or a semicolon at the end of the first clause.

5. d. It is preferable that sentences use an active voice rather than a passive voice. By changing the order of the words, the subject is the thing doing the action.

6. c. The beginning of the sentence is written in the past tense, so the end of the sentence must also be in past tense. *He's*, which is a contraction for *he is*, is present tense.

7. b. *Too* and *to* are homonyms. *Too* means also, and is not the correct word in this sentence.

8. b. The verb *has* does not agree with the subject *I*, and also shifts the passage from past to present tense. Replacing *has* with *had* corrects these issues.

9. a. A comma is not needed in this sentence.

10. c. The purpose of an introduction is to introduce the topic and catch the reader's attention. This is your chance to make the reader want to continue reading your essay.

Sentence structure refers to the way words are put together to create sentences. It includes the following concepts:

- **Subjects and predicates.** A subject is who or what the sentence is about; a predicate is the verb and everything that comes after it. Every complete sentence has a subject and a predicate.
- **Independent and dependent clauses.** A clause is a group of words that includes a subject and a predicate. An independent clause is a complete sentence; a dependent clause is not complete on its own.
- **Fragments and run-ons.** A fragment is an incomplete sentence; a run-on is two complete sentences joined together with a comma or no punctuation at all.
- **Active and passive voice.** In an active voice, the subject of a sentence is doing the action. In a passive voice, the action is being done to the subject.

Usage refers to the rules that determine how words should be used in sentences. It includes the following concepts:

- **Verb conjugation.** A verb's form sometimes changes depending on who's doing the action. For example, we say I want and he wants.
- **Verb tense.** A verb's form changes depending on when it takes place; in the past, present, or future.
- **Subject-verb agreement.** A verb should be made singular or plural to match its subject.

Mechanics are the nuts and bolts of writing, including punctuation, capitalization, and spelling. In regard to punctuation, one of the most important things to study is comma rules. In regard to spelling, you'll need to learn how to use homonyms correctly.

Organization refers to the way sentences and paragraphs are placed in order. There are three major types of organization:

- **Chronological order.** Events are written in the order in which they occurred in time.
- **Order of importance.** Sentences and paragraphs are written in order from least to most important, or vice versa.
- **Cause and effect.** Everything having to do with the cause is written separately from everything having to do with the effect.

On the GED® test, you'll be expected to know when sentences or paragraphs are in the wrong order.

5 ▶ READING AND UNDERSTANDING PASSAGES

CHAPTER SUMMARY

This chapter helps you with the passages that make up the GED® Reasoning through Language Arts test. It teaches you to identify main ideas and supporting details, summarize passages, distinguish fact from opinion, recognize organizational structure, and make inferences.

Older versions of the GED® test contained mostly fiction reading passages. However, the current GED® Reasoning through Language Arts test consists of only about 25% fiction passages. Of these, all will be prose fiction, like the text of a story. Other forms of fiction, such as plays and poems, will no longer be included on the GED® RLA test—the test now focuses on nonfiction.

Nonfiction Passages

Nonfiction passages make up about 75% of all the passages you will see on the GED® Reasoning through Language Arts test. Nonfiction passages also appear on other portions of the GED® test, so improving your ability to read and understand nonfiction passages is key to doing well on the GED® test. Nonfiction can include everything from essays and speeches to instruction manuals and job application letters.

The GED® RLA test focuses on three types of nonfiction reading passages. These have been chosen to ensure that you have an understanding of practical reading and writing situations that you might encounter in the professional world.

Informational Science Passages

These passages will focus on one of two areas within the scientific realm. The first is human health and other biology; this may include topics such as respiration and the interdependence of animal species. The second is energy-related systems; this may include topics such as photosynthesis, climate, and gas combustion.

The emphasis of these passages is not to test you on unfamiliar scientific principles; you will not be expected to provide additional scientific knowledge on the topics presented. These passages will likely focus on your ability to correctly understand the steps in a process, and your ability to explain how the steps relate to each other.

Informational Social Studies Passages

These passages will focus on the theme of the Great American Conversation, which includes discussion of elements of American government and how it relates to society. The passages featured here will likely include excerpts from well-known historical documents, such as the Preamble to the U.S. Constitution, as well as other writings of significant figures in American history. These passages may also include texts from modern-day political figures, and can appear in forms as various as speeches, letters, laws, or diaries.

Informational Workplace Passages

These passages are meant to resemble the kinds of documents you are likely to encounter in a modern workplace setting. These documents may include letters, e-mails, instruction manuals, memos, or lists of policies, among others.

Main Idea and Supporting Details

Every passage you read, regardless of the type of material, has a main idea. The **main idea**, sometimes called the *big idea*, is the central message of the text. To determine the main idea, first identify the topic of the text. Then, think about the major point that the writer is trying to tell readers about the topic. For example, if the topic of a passage is loggerhead sea turtles, the main idea could be as follows:

Loggerhead sea turtles return to the beach where they were born to lay eggs.

This would be the most important idea that the writer wants you to take away from the passage. The rest of the passage would contain information to help explain the main idea. Examples, information, facts, and details that help to explain and describe the main idea are the **supporting details**. These help to strengthen readers' understanding of the main idea.

In the passage about sea turtles, supporting details could include the following sentences:

The turtles crawl onto the beach at night.

They dig a hole in the sand and lay their eggs in the hole.

After covering the nest with sand, the turtles return to the ocean.

Each of these supporting details gives information about the main idea.

There are four basic types of supporting details that writers include to give readers a deeper understanding of the central message of the text. Here are the types of supporting details:

- examples
- reasons

- facts
- descriptions

Being able to identify the main idea and supporting details is helpful in organizing the information in a passage. Readers are able to recognize the central message of the text and identify examples, reasons, facts, and descriptions to clarify and explain the message.

> **TIP**
>
> While the topic of a passage may be as short as a single word, the main idea of a passage is always a complete sentence.

Read the following paragraph. Look for the main idea and supporting details as you read.

> *Before becoming the sixteenth president of the United States, Abraham Lincoln showed a pattern of behavior that caused him to earn the nickname "Honest Abe." Early in his career, he worked in the grocery business. When his partner passed away, leaving behind a mountain of debt, Lincoln not only paid off his own part of the money, but also his late partner's share because this was the honest thing to do. Later, he worked as a lawyer. During that time in history, members of the legal profession were often recognized as being dishonest. However, Lincoln earned the reputation among his colleagues as being a man who never told a lie. He even gave a lecture during which he encouraged the audience to make honesty a priority in their occupations.*

What is the main idea of the passage?

_____

_____

You probably recognized that the first sentence tells the main idea of the passage. You may have stated that the main idea is:

> *Abraham Lincoln earned the nickname "Honest Abe."*
>
> *Abraham Lincoln showed a pattern of honesty throughout his life.*
>
> *People called Lincoln "Honest Abe" because of the priority he placed on honesty.*

Any of these would be correct. The main idea is the most important piece of information, about which the rest of the paragraph is written. Each of these choices captures that information.

Which of the following is a supporting detail from the passage?
   a. Abraham Lincoln was the sixteenth president of the United States.
   b. Lincoln's behavior caused him to be known as "Honest Abe."
   c. Early in his career, Lincoln worked in the grocery business.
   d. Lincoln's colleagues recognized him as a man who never told a lie.

Did you recognize that answer choice **d** supports the main idea of the passage? This statement is an example of the honesty that caused people to call Lincoln "Honest Abe." Choice **b** restates the main idea. Choices **a** and **c** all contain relevant or interesting information, but they do not directly support the main idea, so they are considered minor details rather than supporting details.

What other supporting details are contained in the passage?

_____

_____

Supporting details from the passage include *Lincoln paid off his late partner's debt as well as his own* and *he gave a lecture encouraging the audience to be honest.* These statements support the main idea by giving some reasons why he became known for his honesty.

Some reading passages include more than a single paragraph. Every paragraph will have its own main idea. The main idea is stated in the topic sentence. The **topic sentence** basically sums up what the entire paragraph tries to explain.

Look back at the paragraph about Lincoln. Can you identify the topic sentence? It is the sentence that tells the basic message of the paragraph.

> *Before becoming the sixteenth president of the United States, Abraham Lincoln showed a pattern of behavior that caused him to earn the nickname "Honest Abe."*

This is the first sentence of the paragraph, and it is the topic sentence. Notice that it also contains the main idea. The topic sentence can be anywhere in the paragraph; however, it is generally either the first or last sentence. Being able to locate the topic sentence can be helpful in determining the main idea.

Summarizing

Have you ever given a book report or written a research paper? In either case, you read information from a text, then restated the most important ideas in your own words. This is called **summarizing**.

Being able to summarize information is one way to show how well you understood what you read because it requires you to focus on the main points and explain them. Think back to a research paper you have written. Chances are, you read a number of articles or books about your topic; however, your paper was probably only a few pages long. That's because you only included key pieces of information in your summary. You chose the main idea and the most important supporting details and restated these in the report.

Think back about the paragraph we read about "Honest Abe." What information in the text was the most important? How could you restate that in your own words?

> *Abraham Lincoln was known as "Honest Abe" for many reasons. He showed honesty in his early work life, set an example of honesty as a lawyer working among many dishonest colleagues, and encouraged others to practice honesty as well.*

This summary has two sentences in it. The original paragraph about Lincoln was considerably longer. Because a summary focuses only on the most important information, it is generally much shorter than the original text. In fact, you might summarize an entire book in only a few sentences or paragraphs.

Read the following paragraph.

In the midst of New York Harbor stands a 305-foot tall, 225-ton symbol of freedom and democracy: the Statue of Liberty. "Lady Liberty," as she is affectionately known, was a gift of friendship from France and was dedicated on October 28, 1886. Officially named "The Statue of Liberty Enlightening the World," this highly recognizable structure contains much symbolism. For example, the torch itself is a symbol of enlightenment. The tablet of law held in her left hand contains Roman numerals representing the date of our country's independence, July 4, 1776. Finally, the crown on the head of the statue has seven rays, one for each of the seven continents.

The statue is covered in copper, about the thickness of two pennies. Natural weathering has caused the copper to turn a light green color. When the statue was restored for its 100th birthday, the torch was replaced, and the new torch was covered with a thin layer of 24 karat gold. During the day, the sun's reflection lights the torch; at night, it is lighted by 16 floodlights.

To summarize the passage,

- determine the most important idea.
- decide what information can be left out.
- restate the information using your own words.

Now, let's summarize the passage.

What is the main idea of the entire passage?

_____

What are two important supporting details?

_____

_____

Write a summary of the passage in your own words.

_____

_____

_____

You probably recognized that the main idea is one of the following:

The Statue of Liberty is an important symbol.

The Statue of Liberty is a huge monument that represents many things.

Remember, there is not a single correct way to state the main idea. The important thing is that you recognize which information is the most important.

Next, figure out which supporting details are key. The size of the Statue of Liberty is definitely interesting. It could even be the central idea of another passage. However, in this example, these facts are not some of the supporting details that must find their way into a summary. The same is true about the date the statue was dedicated and the fact that the copper has turned green over the past century and a half. These are ideas that could be left out when you summarize the passage.

The most important supporting details would be those that address the symbolism associated with the statue. Information about the significance of the torch, the tablet, and the crown should be included in a thorough summary.

TIP

Don't forget! A summary must use your own words, not the words of the author. Restate the ideas that you read and make sure you are not copying what is written in the text.

Just like the main idea, there is more than one correct way to summarize a passage. Yours may be similar to the following summary:

> *The Statue of Liberty was a gift from France that symbolizes a number of ideas that are important to our country. The torch represents enlightenment, the tablet recognizes the date of our country's freedom, and the crown acknowledges the seven continents in the world.*

Remember learning that each paragraph has its own main idea? See if you can find the main idea in the second paragraph about "Lady Liberty." If you recognized the main idea as the fact that the Statue of Liberty is coated with a thin layer of copper, you're exactly right! Supporting details include information about the thickness of the copper and the fact that it has changed colors due to weathering.

Remember that understanding the author's purpose is critical to understanding the text itself. If the author's purpose in the previous passage was to persuade readers that the Statue of Liberty was long overdue for restoration, then the supporting details the author chose would probably have focused on the statue's recent state in a negative way. The author might have presented evidence that the structure represented a safety hazard due to its age, or that its weathered copper covering was an eyesore for those who visited it. As written, however, the passage is clearly written to inform the reader.

Fact and Opinion

You probably learned the difference between fact and opinion when you were younger. A **fact** is a true statement that can be proven.

> *California is located on the west coast of the United States.*

This is a fact. Look at any atlas, encyclopedia, or geography book, and you can verify, or prove, that this statement is true.

An **opinion** is a statement that reflects someone's personal views. Not everyone will agree with an opinion.

> *California's beaches are the most beautiful in the whole country.*

Many people would probably agree with this statement. However, this is the writer's personal view. If you were to talk with people sitting on the beaches in Hawaii, North Carolina, or Florida, you'd most likely find at least a few who disagree.

Writers often use a combination of facts and opinions to share their ideas. Being able to distinguish between these statements can help you gain a complete understanding of the passage. Strong readers are able to interpret the information in a passage and form their own opinions.

Four inches of snow fell overnight.

Can this be proven? Absolutely. A ruler or a weather report can be used to check how much snow fell. Because this statement can be proven, it is a fact.

We have had too much snow this winter.

Can this be proven? We could prove that snow has fallen, but how much is too much? Not everyone would agree that there has been too much snow. In fact, some people might think there has not been enough. This statement tells how someone feels about the snow, so it is an opinion.

Facts and opinions are both useful. They not only help writers get their point across; they can be useful to readers as well.

Suppose you want to buy tickets to a play and are trying to decide which play to attend. You would need to know facts such as where each play is being performed, the times and dates of the shows, and the cost of the tickets. These facts are helpful in making up your mind. But, you'll probably want to find some opinions, too. You could read reviews or talk to friends to find out which theaters offer the best seats, which

actors and actresses are the most entertaining, and whether a particular play is completely boring.

The author's purpose for writing a piece can impact whether the text includes mostly facts, mostly opinions, or a combination of both:

- If the author's purpose is *to inform*, the text is likely to contain mostly facts.
- If the author's purpose is *to entertain*, a combination of facts and opinions will be included.
- If the author's purpose is *to persuade*, you can definitely expect to find opinions. However, facts that support or promote the author's opinion may also be included.

As you read the following paragraph, determine which statements are facts and which are opinions. Ask yourself:

1. Can this statement be proven or verified?
2. Would everyone agree with this statement?

The drama club of Meadowbrook Middle School put on a stage presentation of The Elves and the Shoemaker *earlier this month. The students performed before a sold-out crowd for all three performances. The highlight of the evening was a dance by the elves during the second act. Even the principal was seen laughing until tears filled her eyes. It was the first live performance the students put on this year, although plans for a spring musical were announced at the end of the evening. It is sure to be a huge success!*

A woodwind ensemble from the school band provided music before the show as well as during the intermission. This impressive group of young musicians was enjoyed by all. The amazing talent present in the school was obvious in everyone involved, from the actors and actresses to the stagehands and technical crew. Ticket sales for the performances earned nearly $900 for the school's fine arts department.

Did you determine which statements from the review of the play were facts and which were opinions?

Facts from the passage:

- The drama club of Meadowbrook Middle School put on a stage presentation of *The Elves and the Shoemaker* earlier this month.
- The students performed before a sold-out crowd for all three performances.
- Even the principal was seen laughing until tears filled her eyes.
- It was the first live performance the students put on this year, although plans for a spring musical were announced at the end of the evening.
- A woodwind ensemble from the school band provided music before the show as well as during the intermission.
- Ticket sales for the performances earned nearly $900 for the school's fine arts department.

Each of these statements could be proven by checking the school calendar, looking at the program for the performances, or checking with the accountant for the fine arts department. Even the statement about the principal could be verified through a photograph or video. She might even admit it.

Opinions from the passage:

- The highlight of the evening was a dance by the elves during the second act.
- It is sure to be a huge success!
- This impressive group of young musicians was enjoyed by all.
- The amazing talent present in the school was obvious in everyone involved, from the actors and actresses to the stagehands and technical crew.

All these are opinions because there could be people who would not agree with the author. For example, some audience members might have thought the highlight of the evening was when the musicians played, not when the elves danced. Also, *amazing* and *impressive* are words that often indicate an opinion.

Organizational Structure

When you write, whether the text is a story, a letter, or a research paper, you probably spend time planning the order in which you will present your ideas. It would not make sense to randomly write down your thoughts without any pattern or logical order. Before writing, you probably organize similar ideas together or tell actions and events in the order in which they happened. Without using some sort of organization, not only would you have trouble getting your thoughts across accurately, but your readers would also become terribly confused.

Writers want their texts to make sense. The whole point of writing is to share information and ideas with an audience, and writers carefully consider how to best arrange this information so that readers are able to follow their thoughts and fully understand the passage. The **organizational structure** of a passage is the way a writer arranges his or her ideas.

Common types of organizational structures that writers may choose include *sequence*, *cause and effect*, *compare and contrast*, *problem and solution*, *classification*, and *description*.

Understanding how information is presented can help readers

- organize and understand the passage.
- anticipate what ideas might be presented next.
- think about what information to look for.
- make predictions.
- connect ideas from different parts of the text.

To recognize which organizational structure an author has used, think about what he or she wants readers to know. If an author wants to be sure readers understand the order in which events occurred, sequence is probably used. If he or she wants readers to know what led up to a particular event, a cause and effect structure is likely to be found. Recognizing and understanding each type of organizational structure can make a big difference in how well you comprehend the material.

Now, let's talk about each type of organizational structure in a little more detail.

Sequence

The **sequence** of events is the order in which the events are discussed in a passage. When readers are able to recognize that a text uses a sequential organizational structure, they know that details, ideas, and events will be presented in a specific order. Often, the sequence used is either time order or order of importance.

Time order means that ideas and events are presented chronologically, or in the order in which they actually happened. Often, words and phrases such as the following indicate time order:

- first
- second
- next
- then
- last

- before
- after that
- following
- by the time
- as soon as

Writers often use time order when the correct order is important. For example, history books are often written in time order by beginning with the earliest events and leading up to the most recent. Correct order would also be important when readers are expected to follow steps in a particular sequence, such as directions, how-to articles, and recipes.

Of all days for it to happen, my alarm clock didn't go off this morning. As soon as I opened my eyes and saw sunlight, I knew it would be a race to make it to the bus on time. The first thing I did was jump in the shower, wash my hair quickly, then jump right back out. Next was the dash to the closet. Shirt on, jeans zipped, shoes tied, and down the stairs. By the time I reached the kitchen, Mom had my peanut butter toast wrapped in a napkin and ready to go. I ran out the door, and before it even slammed behind me, the bus pulled up to the curb. Yes! I made it!

The transition words in the paragraph help readers know exactly when each action happened. On the lines below, list the events of the paragraph in the correct order.

_____

_____

_____

_____

You probably figured out that the events occurred in this order:

1. The alarm clock did not go off.
2. The speaker opened his or her eyes.
3. The speaker showered.
4. The speaker got dressed.
5. Mom wrapped up the toast in a napkin.
6. The speaker ran out the door.
7. The bus reached the curb.
8. The door slammed.

Another sequence writers may use to organize their writing is by **order of importance**. They might choose to tell the most important idea first, followed by ideas that decrease in importance. This is a good way to catch the readers' attention by beginning with the strongest point.

Did you know that newspaper articles are often organized in order of importance? The most important information is usually listed at the beginning of the article, followed by less important information. The reason for this is that some readers do not take the time to finish the entire article. This organizational structure ensures that those readers do not miss the most important ideas.

Conversely, writers may begin by telling the least important idea, then list ideas or events in increasing order of importance, telling the most important idea last. This leaves readers with the strongest point freshest in their minds.

The Tri-City Tigers won the district soccer championship on Friday night! The final score was 5–2 in what was a very exciting game. Jackson Greenwood scored three goals for the

Tigers. Coach Abbott placed each team member in the game at some point. It was truly a victory for all!

The fact that the Tigers won the championship is the most important idea in the paragraph, so it is stated at the beginning. The final score is the second most important piece of information, so it is stated next. Jackson scoring two goals is next in importance, followed by the fact that all the players were involved in the win.

If the writer had chosen to tell the events in order of least to most importance, the paragraph could have been organized as shown here:

All members of the Tigers soccer team got a chance to play in Friday night's game, thanks to Coach Abbott. Jackson Greenwood scored three goals for his team. The final score of the exciting game was 5–2, giving the Tri-City Tigers the title of district champs!

Cause and Effect

As you know, a *cause* is something that makes something else happen. An *effect* is what happens as a result of the cause. For example, if you go to bed late, you'll be tired in the morning. Going to bed late is the cause; being tired in the morning is the effect.

At times, there is a cause and effect relationship between events in a passage. Authors may choose to use a **cause and effect** organizational structure, which focuses on such relationships, in the text. Recognizing a cause and effect structure lets readers know that they should be on the lookout for things that are the result of a given event. It also helps readers understand how events in the passage are related to one another.

Darnell studied every night for a week, so he got an A on his science exam.

How are these events related? Did one thing happen as a result of the other? Yes. Studying every night *caused* Darnell to do well on the test. He got an A *because* he studied so much. So, studying every night is the cause; getting an A on the exam is the effect.

Often, writers will include clues—words that signal a cause and effect relationship. Examples of such words are listed here:

- because
- then
- as a result

- so
- due to
- therefore

- since
- when
- if

> *Ella fixed French toast for breakfast since it was her parents' anniversary.*

In this sentence, the clue word *since* indicates a cause and effect relationship. In the sentence about Darnell, the clue word *so* signaled the relationship.

Notice that either the cause or the effect can come first. In Darnell's example, the cause is first; in Ella's example, the effect is first. To determine which event is the cause and which is the effect, ask yourself which event is the result of the other.

Now it's your turn. Read the following paragraph. As you read, look for cause and effect relationships.

> *During the past quarter, our company had a record number of sales. As a result, we also saw a significant increase in profits. So, over the next few weeks, we will be able to hire additional employees in several departments to take on some of the workload. Current employees will also receive a bonus in their next paycheck as recognition for their contribution to our company's continued success.*

What signal words were included to offer clues about the cause and effect relationships?

_____

As a result and *so* were used to highlight two of the relationships. However, you probably noticed that more than two relationships existed. Signal words are not always included. Be sure to read carefully and think about how the events in a passage are related, whether signal words are included or not.

Did you recognize all the cause and effect relationships in this paragraph?

The *cause*:

- a record number of sales for the company

The *effects*:

- a significant increase in profits
- the hiring of additional employees
- a bonus for current employees

Notice that a single cause had more than one effect. The opposite may also be true; a single effect can be the result of several causes.

Compare and Contrast

When we *compare*, we tell how two or more things are alike. When we *contrast*, we tell how two or more things are different. Writers often use a **compare and contrast** organizational structure to explain ideas, events, people, or objects by describing the ways in which they are alike or different. When readers recognize a compare and contrast structure in a passage, they look for similarities and differences between the topics.

Signal words often alert readers that things are alike or different in some way.

Similarities
- also
- like
- both
- alike
- similar
- likewise
- the same as
- at the same time
- in the same ways
- in the same manner

Differences
- but
- yet
- only
- differ
- unlike
- rather
- although
- however
- different
- less than
- better than
- nevertheless
- on the contrary

By comparing and contrasting, writers are able to help readers gain a clear understanding of their ideas.

Chinchillas are small animals that are slightly larger and rounder than squirrels. Both animals are generally gray or brown in color. The chinchilla often has a bushy tail similar to that of a squirrel, although its ears are more round, like those of a mouse.

The comparisons and contrasts in this paragraph help describe chinchillas in a way that gives readers a clear picture of these animals.

What signal words did you notice in the paragraph?

_____

You probably recognized that *slightly larger and rounder than*, *both*, *similar to*, *although*, and *like* pointed out similarities and differences between the various animals.

There are two types of compare and contrast organizational structures that writers often use. **Whole-to-whole comparisons** completely discuss the first idea, event, or item and then completely discuss the second. For example, if a writer were comparing and contrasting sports, he might completely explain baseball, then completely describe soccer.

Part-to-part comparisons discuss one particular aspect of each topic, then discuss another aspect, and so on. For example, a writer might discuss the number of players on baseball and soccer teams, then discuss how points are scored in each game, and then discuss the rules for each game.

Problem and Solution

If an author elects to use a **problem and solution** organizational structure, a problem is discussed and is then followed by one or more solutions to the problem. When readers recognize this structure, they know that as they read, they should look for possible ways to solve the problem.

Construction of the new auditorium at Forest Lakes Middle School is scheduled to begin in early April, which will interfere with the school's planned Spring Fling Carnival because construction equipment will occupy a large portion of the area normally used for the event. The carnival committee believes it may be possible to reschedule the carnival for the middle of March, prior to groundbreaking on the construction project. If that is not possible, the committee may consider moving some of the activities indoors, reducing the need for some of the outside space. It has also been suggested that an alternative location, such as the nearby Little League fields, be used for the event.

What problem is the topic of the paragraph?

_____

The problem is that there may not be enough space for the school carnival after construction has begun on the new auditorium.

What solutions are suggested?

_____

_____

_____

Three possible solutions are suggested: change the date of the carnival, move some of the activities indoors, and change the location of the event. In a longer passage, the problem might be introduced in one paragraph, with each solution being discussed in separate paragraphs.

Classification

Sometimes, writers divide information about a topic into smaller sections that each focus on a group of related ideas or objects. This organizational structure is called **classification**, and writers use it to arrange ideas and information into categories. Each category contains ideas that are similar in some way.

Readers can recognize that classification has been used if the passage talks about different kinds of things, such as different kinds of animals, different types of transportation, or different kinds of sports. This structure lets readers know that ideas in each section will be somehow related.

TIP

Sometimes, section headers will be a clue that the organizational structure is classification. For example, a passage about animals might include section headers such as *mammals*, *reptiles*, *birds*, *amphibians*, and *fish*.

Dear Friends,

We are pleased that you are planning a trip to our resort! We are sure that you will find the vacation package that best suits your needs. Vacation packages are grouped into three categories. You may make your selection at any time prior to your arrival.

Room-only packages include your hotel room and access to the resort's three swimming pools. You may also enjoy the exercise equipment in the gym at no additional charge.

Bed-and-breakfast packages include your hotel room as well as access to the pools and gym. Breakfast in any of the resort restaurants is also included, or you may choose to order your morning meal from our room service menu.

All-inclusive packages include not only the offerings of the previous packages, but also lunch and dinner from any of the resort restaurants or room service. Each guest may enjoy three meals and two snacks each day, all included in the price of the package.

We look forward to your stay and would be happy to answer any questions. Feel free to contact us at any time for further assistance.

Sincerely,

Resort Manager

This passage uses a classification organizational structure. What is the topic of the letter?

_____

What were the categories that the information was divided into?

_____

You probably recognized that the topic is the resort's vacation packages, and the categories the packages are divided into include *room-only*, *bed-and-breakfast*, and *all-inclusive* options.

Description

When an author chooses a **description** as the organizational pattern for a passage, he or she will introduce the topic, then discuss attributes and characteristics that describe it. When readers recognize this organizational pattern, they know to anticipate finding details, attributes, examples, and characteristics that will help explain the topic.

> *For more than 200 years, the White House has been home to the presidents of the United States and is undoubtedly the most recognizable residence in the country. A view of the front reveals a two-story structure with rows of rectangular windows, columns in the center of the building, and our nation's flag flying over the roof. Indoors, the home boasts six levels, including 132 rooms, 35 restrooms, and 28 fireplaces. For recreation, the First Family can enjoy a tennis court, jogging track, swimming pool, movie theater, and bowling alley, all without leaving the comfort of their very famous home.*

In this paragraph, the topic was introduced in the first sentence. The following sentences describe what the White House looks like from the outside, the structure of the inside, and the recreational features of the building. Each of these details helps give the reader a clear picture of the topic.

Inferences

Sometimes, writers come right out and directly state everything they want readers to know. Other times, a writer will make suggestions about a person, place, event, or object without directly stating the information. To gain a complete understanding of the passage, readers have to read between the lines and construct meaning about the information in the text. An educated guess based on clues in the passage is an **inference**.

To make an inference, consider

- clues and hints in the passage.
- your own prior knowledge.
- observations.
- details in the text.

Making inferences is similar to drawing conclusions.

When readers make inferences, they recognize ideas that are implied.

> *Elliot showed his little brother around the school, making sure he would be able to find his locker, classrooms, and most importantly, the cafeteria.*

What information is implied in this sentence? Based on what we read, what we already know, and what makes logical sense, we can infer several things:

> *Elliot's brother is unfamiliar with the school.*
>
> *Elliot's brother is a new student.*
>
> *Elliot already attends the school.*

These ideas were not directly stated. However, if we read between the lines, we can infer that they are most likely true.

TIP

Keep in mind that inferences are not random, wild guesses. They are based on information that you have been given as well as what you already know. Inferences are *logical* conclusions.

BOOST

Did you know that about 71% of people who take the GED® test have already reached at least grade 10? Comedian Bill Cosby left high school in grade 10, passed his GED® test, then went on to Temple University. In fact, one in ten college freshmen earn their GED® test credential before arriving on campus!

At times, you will have to make inferences to determine different things about a passage, such as the main idea, purpose, tone, or point of view. You will have to pay attention to the details in the text to infer this information.

To gain a complete understanding of the text, readers may have to make **multiple inferences** by considering information from various parts of the text. This requires readers to think about their purpose for reading, evaluate the importance of ideas and details, then decide what information is key to understanding what the writer wants them to know about the passage.

For example, suppose you are reading a passage describing how to make a birdhouse. Based on the purpose of the text, you know that it is essential to find the steps necessary to complete the project. If you came across information describing why birds migrate in the winter, you could categorize these facts as being unimportant to the purpose of this particular passage. If you came across information telling you to first measure a piece of wood, you would know that this detail is essential in understanding the text.

Readers also might need to consider information from various parts of the text to make strong predictions. Think of each piece of information as a piece to a jigsaw puzzle. The more pieces you have, the better equipped you will be to predict what the finished puzzle will look like. Consider each piece of information as it relates to what you have already read. Then, use this combination of ideas to infer what is likely to happen next in the text.

Considering all the pieces of information in a passage can also be helpful in making inferences about the author. What authors say, as well as what they do not say, can help readers recognize their attitudes, beliefs, biases, prejudgments, and opinions about the topic.

Four bands performed at the school's Winter Wonderland Formal. The ultimate hip-hop band Sticks and Stones rocked the crowd first. Nearly every student was on the dance floor the entire time they played. The drumbeat of their signature hit "Keep Movin'" undoubtedly stuck in everyone's heads for days. After their set, the bands Golden Child, Harvey's Dudes, and Stumped also played.

Which inference could be made about the passage?
a. The author is the drummer in a hip-hop band.
b. Sticks and Stones was the audience's favorite musical group.
c. Nearly all the students attended the Winter Wonderland Formal.
d. The author believes Sticks and Stones was the best band at the dance.

The author's opinion about the bands is obvious. You could probably read between the lines and infer that the author really enjoyed the performance by Sticks and Stones. Think about all the words and details he or she included when talking about the band. Then, think about what he or she *didn't* say; the author only quickly mentioned the other bands, without giving any information about the bands or their performances. Choice **d** is the best answer.

Making Comparisons between Passages

A number of questions on the GED® Reasoning through Language Arts test will involve comparing two passages that contain related ideas. For example, the text of Lincoln's Emancipation Proclamation might be followed by an excerpt from a speech by Confederate President Jefferson Davis regarding slavery. In this case, the two passages provide opposing viewpoints of a single issue. In other cases, the passages might deal with the same idea or theme but offer differences in style, tone, or even purpose. In any case, the most important questions to ask when comparing two passages are:

In what ways are the two passages similar?
In what ways are the two passages different?

When two passages are paired together, you will often encounter a question about the main idea or theme that is common to both passages. If you can identify the ways in which the two passages are similar, this will help you determine whether they share a single idea or theme. When two passages are placed together on the GED® test, you can be sure that they are related in some way—it's up to you to figure out exactly how they are related.

When comparing passages, remember to look at both the content and the form of the passages. Two passages with dramatically different forms, such as an e-mail and a news article, might actually contain the same main idea but differ in structure, style, tone, or intended audience. By contrast, two passages that are both excerpted from persuasive essays might share the same form, style, and intended audience, but offer opposing arguments and evidence on a topic.

For the extended response item on the GED® Reasoning through Language Arts test, you may be required to write a short essay comparing two passages that contain related ideas. When writing, it is especially important to mention the specific details in each passage that support the main idea. You may even want to quote small amounts of text from each passage to support your analysis. Be careful to avoid drawing comparisons between elements that are not important to the main idea or theme. For example, two passages may both be written in an informal style, but unless that style is important to understanding the author's purpose, it should not be brought up as a key point in your response.

Quiz

Now that you've had a chance to review some of the skills needed to comprehend nonfiction, read each of the following passages, then choose the one best answer to each question.

Directions: Choose the *one best answer* to each question.

Questions 1 through 5 refer to the following passage.

What Is Included in a Healthy Diet?

Most people recognize the importance of a healthy lifestyle. Part of this includes enjoying a balanced diet. Each day, people need to eat foods from each food group to

(5) be sure they are getting the benefits offered by each type of food.

It is recommended that people enjoy between 6 and 11 servings of food from the grain food group. These foods include

(10) bread, rice, pasta, and cereal. Those made from whole grains offer the most health benefits. Enjoying whole grain toast for breakfast, a sandwich on a wheat pita for lunch, and whole wheat pasta for dinner are

(15) ways to ensure that plenty of servings of these foods have found their way onto our plates.

We all know the benefits of eating plenty
of fruits and vegetables, but do we

(20) really get enough every day? It is recommended that people enjoy three to five servings of vegetables and three to four servings of fruit every day. That may sound like a lot, but whipping up a fruit smoothie

(25) at the beginning of the day, having veggies and dip as a snack, and adding fresh berries to a yogurt parfait for dessert are ways to think outside of the box—a box of fruit snacks, that is.

(30) Getting enough protein doesn't have to mean eating two to three burgers each day. Did you know that beans, eggs, and nuts are considered protein as well? Sure, a burger, fish, chicken, or steak would be great at

(35) lunch or dinner, but including eggs at breakfast or a handful of almonds in the afternoon can cut down on the amount of meat in your diet, while still guaranteeing the protein your body needs.

(40) We all know the importance of dairy for strong teeth and bones. But don't feel that you have to drown yourself in skim milk to get your two to three servings a day. Remember that fruit and yogurt parfait?

(45) That's a yummy way to get a full serving of dairy. And how about the grilled cheese sandwich on wheat for lunch? Cheese is another way to get some dairy into your diet.

Eating a balance of food from each

(50) group is essential to staying healthy and feeling your best. Remember to mix it up. Try new things and be sure to get the servings you need each day.

1. Which statement from the passage is an opinion?
   a. Most people recognize the importance of a healthy lifestyle.
   b. Those made from whole grains offer the most health benefits.
   c. That's a yummy way to get a full serving of dairy.
   d. Cheese is another way to get some dairy into your diet.

2. Which organizational structure is used in the passage?
   a. sequence
   b. classification
   c. cause and effect
   d. problem and solution

3. What is the main idea of the passage?
   a. We need to include plenty of dairy in our diets.
   b. Most foods can be grouped into five basic types.
   c. A balanced diet is an important part of a healthy lifestyle.
   d. There are creative ways to be sure we eat the right nutrients.

4. Which detail supports the main idea of the third paragraph?
   a. A fruit smoothie can help us get enough servings of fruit.
   b. A box of fruit snacks offers an entire serving of fresh fruit.
   c. We all know the benefits of eating plenty of fruits and vegetables.
   d. We need between six and nine servings of vegetables and fruits daily.

5. Which choice best summarizes the passage?
   a. A balanced diet includes plenty of grains, fruits and vegetables, dairy, and protein to help us stay healthy. These foods can be incorporated into our diets in creative ways throughout the day.
   b. Protein and dairy are important foods that come from many sources. Meats, nuts, and eggs offer our bodies the protein we need, while milk, yogurt, and cheese give us dairy for strong bones and teeth.
   c. Eating the right kinds of foods is important to staying healthy. Exercise, plenty of sleep, and eating a balanced diet ensure that we have enough energy every day as well as the nutrients we need to build muscles.
   d. Each day, we need 6 to 11 servings of grains, especially whole grains. We can get these nutrients from breads, cereals, rice, and pasta. Including these foods at every meal will ensure that we get enough of them.

Questions 6 through 10 refer to the following passage.

What Types of Jobs Are Available?
Currently, Fairhaven Fine Furnishings has a job opening available in the warehouse. Daily job requirements include unloading trucks of furniture and accessories delivered
(5) by the manufacturers, organizing these items in the warehouse, locating and preparing items to fill customer orders, and loading these items onto our company's trucks for delivery. This job requires
(10) employees to be able to lift at least 100 pounds, operate a forklift, and demonstrate exceptional record-keeping abilities, as maintaining accurate inventory is of utmost importance. This job offers many
(15) opportunities for future advancement within the company. Many of Fairhaven's current management team members began their careers working in the warehouse. This is a full-time position, paying $17.75 per hour.
(20) Health insurance, including vision and dental benefits, will be available after 90 days, assuming the employee receives an acceptable performance evaluation at that point.
(25)   Fairhaven Fine Furnishings also has openings available for a data entry clerk and a receptionist. Both positions require exceptional computer skills, and applicants will need to demonstrate adequate abilities
(30) prior to being hired. The receptionist must also have excellent communication and customer service skills, as he or she will be responsible for answering phone calls and greeting customers as they enter our
(35) showroom. Likewise, the data entry clerk must demonstrate strong communication skills, as this position requires interacting with company representatives from our various departments as well as

(40) representatives from each of the companies
       that provide our products. However, the data
       entry clerk will not be communicating
       directly with Fairhaven's customers. The
       receptionist position is full-time and pays
(45) $10.50 per hour. The data entry position is
       20 hours per week and pays $12.35 per hour.
       Both positions include health insurance
       benefits following an acceptable 90-day
       performance evaluation. The company will
(50) also contribute toward vision and dental
       benefits, making a greater contribution
       toward these benefits for full-time employees
       than those working part-time.
             Applicants for any of these positions
(55) must first submit a completed resume,
       including work and salary history, and a list
       of three professional references. After these
       documents have been reviewed by a
       department manager, qualified applicants
(60) will be contacted for a telephone interview.
       The final step in the hiring process will be a
       personal interview with our hiring team.

6. Based on the passage, which of these statements
   is a fact?
   a. Fairhaven Fine Furnishings would be a great
      place to work.
   b. The receptionist position is better suited for
      a woman than a man.
   c. All the available positions offer some health
      insurance benefits.
   d. The phone interview is the most important
      step in the hiring process.

7. What is the organizational structure of the first
   paragraph?
   a. sequential
   b. description
   c. cause and effect
   d. problem and solution

8. Which is true about the second and third
   paragraphs?
   a. The second paragraph uses classification to
      group similar ideas.
   b. The steps in the application process are
      listed in a random order.
   c. Signal words indicate a cause and effect
      structure in the paragraphs.
   d. Two job positions are compared and
      contrasted in the second paragraph.

9. Which inference can best be made, based on
   the information in the passage?
   a. The data entry clerk is the most important
      position.
   b. Warehouse employees are valued very highly
      within the company.
   c. The company is likely to hire the first
      applicant for each of the jobs.
   d. The receptionist position will be the most
      difficult for the company to fill.

10. What is the main idea of the third paragraph?
   a. Some applicants will be invited to interview
      in person.
   b. There are several steps involved in the hiring
      process.
   c. Department managers will contact qualified
      applicants by phone.
   d. Only the most qualified applicants will meet
      with the hiring team.

Answers

1. c. Not everyone would agree that a certain food is *yummy*, which makes this statement an opinion. The other answer choices all include statements that could be proven. Most people do know that a healthy lifestyle is important, and the information about whole grains and cheese could be verified in a health or science textbook.

2. b. The types of foods needed to stay healthy are classified by similarities. Each of the food groups discussed is a category. Information about the types of food in each category, as well as the number of servings needed daily, is included in that section of the text.

3. c. The importance of a balanced diet is the main point that the author wants readers to understand. Including plenty of dairy is a detail that supports the main idea. While it is true that most foods can be grouped into five basic types, this is not the main point of the passage.

4. d. Choice **d** states the main idea of the third paragraph, and the statement that fruit smoothies are one way to get enough servings of fruit supports this idea. Fruit snacks are mentioned in the passage, but nothing is said about them actually offering a serving of fruit. Choice **c** is also a statement from the passage; however, it does not support the main idea.

5. a. Choice **a** restates the main idea and the most important details from the passage. Choice **b** summarizes the third and fourth paragraphs, while choice **d** summarizes the second paragraph. The information in choice **c** is true; however, it includes information that was not mentioned in the paragraph.

6. c. By reading the job descriptions, we can prove that each position offers insurance benefits. Because the statement can be verified, it is a fact. Not everyone would agree with the other three answer choices, so they are opinions.

7. b. The topic of this paragraph is the warehouse employee position. This topic is introduced in the beginning of the paragraph, then the remainder of the sentences describe the position. The requirements, hours, salary, and benefits are all explained. The order of the information is not important, there is not a problem to discuss, and no events result in the occurrence of other events.

8. d. The words *both* and *likewise* indicate ways in which the two jobs are similar. *However, on the other hand,* and *greater* point out differences between the two positions. The third paragraph uses a sequential organizational structure, listing the steps in the order in which they will occur. *First, after,* and *final* are clues to the structure used in this paragraph.

9. b. Several clues help you read between the lines in this passage. Notice that the warehouse employee receives a much higher salary and more benefits than the others. Also, the passage states that the warehouse job "offers many opportunities for future advancement" and that "many of Fairhaven's current management team members began their careers working in the warehouse." Such advancement is not mentioned for either of the other available positions. These hints indicate that warehouse employees are valued highly within the company.

10. b. The main idea of this paragraph is implied rather than directly stated. Readers are able to infer this information by reading the entire paragraph. Although it is not the main idea, readers can also infer the idea that only the most qualified applicants will meet with the hiring team in person because the other steps seem to narrow down the field to only those best suited for the job. Choices **a, c,** and **d,** are supporting details.

In this chapter, you learned several strategies to help you better comprehend nonfiction reading materials:

1. The main idea is the central message of a passage. Supporting details help to strengthen readers' understanding of the main idea.

2. To summarize is to restate the most important information in your own words. Be sure to think about the main idea and the most important details when creating a summary.

3. Writers include both facts and opinions to express their ideas. Facts are provable and can be verified; opinions tell someone's personal thoughts or ideas, may vary from one person to another, and cannot be verified.

4. Organizational structure refers to the way ideas are arranged in a passage. Common structures include sequence, cause and effect, compare and contrast, problem and solution, classification, and description.

5. When sequence is used to organize a passage, ideas may be listed in time order or in order of importance. Writers may choose to begin with either the most important or least important idea.

6. A cause and effect structure points out how ideas or events are related. A cause is the reason another event occurs; an effect is the result of one or more causes.

7. To compare is to show how ideas, events, or objects are similar; to contrast is to point out ways in which the topics are different. A compare and contrast structure focuses on these similarities and differences.

8. A problem and solution structure introduces a problem, then discusses one or more possibie ways to solve the problem.

9. When a writer uses classification as the organizational structure, he or she groups similar ideas together in categories.

10. A description introduces a topic, then provides information and details to explain the topic to readers.

11. To make an inference means to read between the lines and determine what the writer is telling readers without directly stating that information.

12. At times, readers will need to make multiple inferences to fully understand a passage. This may require putting together bits of information located throughout the text to figure out what the writer wants readers to understand.

CHAPTER

6 ▶ READING TIPS AND STRATEGIES

CHAPTER SUMMARY
This chapter covers GED® test reading tips and strategies that will help you be successful on exam day. You'll learn how to read each kind of passage effectively and efficiently, how to select and eliminate answers, and how to manage your time during the test. This chapter also contains stress management strategies for the days before and the day of the real test.

Throughout this book, you've learned about the types of materials you'll find on the GED® Reasoning through Language Arts test, and you've reviewed the strategies that will help you best comprehend the passages. In this chapter, we discuss some general tips for taking the test as well as some useful tips for each type of passage you will read.

Reading the Passages

Keep in mind that you will be reading several passages on the test.

Pay Attention to the Purpose Question

As you already know, each passage is preceded by a purpose question. This question is printed in bold and is there to give you a purpose and focus as you read. Use this question to your benefit. Read it carefully, and think about what you might read about in the passage.

Suppose the following is one of the purpose questions on your test:

Who Is Knocking?

How can this help you? Well, before you even begin reading, you know that in the passage, you will read about someone knocking. Because the purpose question doesn't tell you who that is, you know you need to look for that information as you read. For some reason, this is going to be important for you to know.

> The purpose question is just there to provide a focus for your reading; you will not have to answer this question.

Read the Questions First

Another way to help you focus on important information as you read a passage is to take a quick look at the questions *before* you begin reading. This will help you know what information to look for in the passage.

1. How does the author feel about the topic?

By reading the questions ahead of time, you know you need to look for words and details that offer clues about the author's attitude toward the subject matter. This could help focus your attention as you read and possibly save time in the long run.

First Scan, Then Read

You may find it helpful to quickly scan the passage to identify the main idea, then go back and read the passage carefully. Knowing the main idea first can help

you identify supporting details as you read. This also lets you know what information you should be looking for when you read the passage slowly and critically the second time.

Read Carefully

Make sure you read slowly and carefully enough to catch every single detail. You may be a master at skimming a passage to simply get the gist of it, but now is not the time to practice that skill. Really focus on the material and think about what you are reading.

Use Context Clues

Don't get upset if you come across an unfamiliar word in a passage. Use what you have learned about context clues to figure out the meaning. Try doing the following:

- Notice how the word is used in the sentence.
- Read the surrounding sentences.
- Look for hints such as synonyms, antonyms, examples, and definitions.
- Think about what would make sense in the context of the passage.

To correctly answer the questions, it is imperative that you completely understand each passage.

Notice Important Details

As you read, pay attention to words, phrases, and details that seem to be important to the meaning of the passage. Be on the lookout for the information listed here:

- key words
- names of real people
- names of characters
- names of locations
- dates
- headings
- specific details
- clues about mood or tone
- hints about the theme
- point of view

Read Everything

As you read, you may come across information that is set off in brackets. These are explanatory notes that can provide valuable information.

Information in brackets [such as these] can be helpful in selecting the best answer.

It may be tempting to skip over the information in the brackets, especially if you're beginning to feel the time crunch. Don't skip anything. Be sure to read all the information you've been given. It may be there for a good reason.

Classify Information

As you read, be sure to recognize the difference between the main idea and supporting details. Also, be sure to recognize whether a statement is a fact or an opinion. Classifying statements correctly can help you completely understand the passage and mentally organize the ideas you have read.

Don't Forget the Visuals

Any time a passage includes visual displays, pay close attention to them! They are probably there for a reason and often include extremely valuable information that will deepen your understanding of the passage. Visual aids that you might find include the following:

- maps
- charts
- graphs
- diagrams
- illustrations
- photographs

Read the titles, labels, and captions as well as the information contained within the visuals themselves.

Read the Passage Completely

Some people find it helpful to read the questions before reading the passage. That's great; however, you need to read the passage completely before trying to actually *answer* the questions, even if the questions appear to be simple. Most of the questions will require you to understand the entire passage completely in order to correctly answer them. Remember, this is not the time to assume that you know what the passage is about. Read the entire text carefully, then answer the questions.

Carefully Read the Questions

This may seem obvious, but it is vital that you read each question carefully and make sure you completely understand exactly what is being asked. In fact, read each question twice. How can you select the correct answer if you misread or do not understand the question?

Which of the following is least likely to occur next?

Suppose you read this question too quickly. You might miss the word *least*. This one simple word completely changes the question. Overlooking one word in a question could cause you to select the wrong answer choice.

Also, it may be tempting to assume that you know what the question is asking, especially if several similar questions are grouped together and you're feeling rushed for time. But remember—just because it would be logical for a certain question to come next, there's no guarantee that it will.

Pay Attention to Line Numbers

Some questions may refer to line numbers in the passage. Be sure to refer back to the passage and read the information in that line again. It is important to understand the words and information in the correct context.

> *What is the meaning of the word* buffet *in line 17?*

You're probably familiar with the word *buffet* and could easily give a definition. But, this word does have several meanings. Without reading line 17, how will you know which meaning is correct?

> (17) *Heavy raindrops and hail continued to buffet the tiny cabin throughout the night.*

Now that you've read the word in the correct context, you will be able to select the appropriate meaning.

Pay Attention to Information in the Question

The question itself may offer essential information that you will need in order to select the best answer choice. Synthesis questions, for example, require you to combine information provided in the question with information in the passage.

Other questions may refer to a specific quotation or section of the passage. If so, there's a pretty good chance that the answer can be found in or near that section. The reference is there for a reason.

TIP

Any information that is offered within a question is important! It would not be there if you didn't need it.

Selecting the Best Answer

You know all the reasons why test takers should read the passages and questions carefully. Now comes the part that makes all the difference: selecting the best answer. When all is said and done, this is the part of the test that matters most. To do well on the GED® test, it is essential that you select the best possible answer to each question.

Try to Answer the Question before Reading the Choices

As soon as you finish reading the question, think about what the best answer would be. Then, see if your answer is among the choices listed. If so, there's a good chance that it is correct, but don't mark the answer right away. Read all the choices first to be sure your answer is really the most complete option.

Read Every Choice

As you read the answer choices, you may determine that the first choice looks really great. But don't stop there! Read every single choice, no matter how wonderful any one of them appears to be. You may find that one of the first answers looks good but that the last one is even better.

Read Each Choice Carefully

Remember how important it is to be sure you read every single word in a question? The same holds true for reading each answer choice. Read each choice slowly and carefully, paying attention to every word. Take the time to read each answer choice twice before making your selection. Slight differences in wording can make one answer choice better than the others.

Use the Information in the Passage

Make sure that you choose an answer based solely on the information in the passage. You may already know a lot about the topic, which is great; however, the correct answers are in the passage. This test is not asking about what you knew before you read the material; it only wants to find out whether you are able to identify the correct information in this text.

Avoid Careless Mistakes

There will probably be answers you know right off the bat. Don't rush on these. Even if a question appears to be easy, read the question and answer choices carefully before making your selection. Careless mistakes can lower your score.

Watch Out for Absolutes

If certain words are found in answer choices, they should catch your attention. Look for words such as these:

- always
- never
- forever
- every

It is unlikely that the correct answer choice includes these inflexible words. Very few things are *always* true or *never* occur. Be suspicious if an answer choice suggests otherwise.

Pay Attention to Except and Not

Be sure you read every word in a question and pay close attention to the words *except* and *not*. It is easy to overlook these words by reading too quickly, and they completely change the question.

One trick for correctly answering these questions is to cover *except* or *not*, read the question, then look for the answer choice that does *not* belong.

Read Each Question for What It Is

Have you ever read a test question and wondered, *"What is this* really *asking?"* It can be easy to read too much into a question. Try not to do that on this test. The good news is, there are no trick questions on the GED® test. Just pay attention to what is being asked and select the best answer.

Choose the Best Answer

As you look through all the answer choices, you may find that more than one could be correct. Make sure that the answer you choose *most completely* answers the question. Just because a statement is true or looks like an acceptable choice does not mean it is the *best* answer. Carefully evaluate each choice before making a selection. Also, make sure your choice is the best answer *based on the passage*, not based on your own assumptions or beliefs.

> **TIP**
>
> Tempting answer choices are often listed before the best answer choice. Read all the answers carefully and make sure you completely understand each option before selecting the best response.

Read the Question Again

After you have selected your answer, read the question one more time. Make sure that your choice actually answers the question that was asked. Read the question, the appropriate section of the passage, and any visual aids, then read your answer choice. Does your answer make sense? If so, great! If not, now is your chance to try again.

Trust Your Instincts

Did you know that your first answer is usually correct? If you know that you have carefully read the passage and each answer choice, you have probably selected your best choice.

You may have time at the end of the test to look back over some of your answers. Unless you find an obvious mistake that you are certain about, don't change your answers. Research has shown that your first answer is usually right.

Answer Every Question

Make sure you do not leave any answers blank. Any question that is not answered is considered wrong, so take your best guess. There is no guessing penalty, so it is better to guess than to not answer a question.

BOOST

If you have been diagnosed as having a learning disability or physical handicap, you may be entitled to special accommodations for taking the GED® test. Be sure to check with the testing center you will be attending ahead of time to find out what, if any, documentation you might need to provide.

Eliminating Answer Choices

There may be times when you have no idea which answer choice is correct, and your only option is to take your best guess. In this situation, it is important to eliminate as many incorrect answer choices as possible, then select among those that remain.

Think of it this way: If you randomly choose one of the four answer choices, you have a 1 in 4 chance of getting it right. That's a 25% chance. Not bad, but definitely not in your best interest.

Suppose you are able to eliminate one of the answer choices. Now, you have a 1 in 3 chance of guessing correctly. Your odds just increased to 33%. Eliminate two choices and you have a 1 in 2 chance of answering correctly. This 50% chance of getting the answer right is much better than what you started with. Now, your random guess is much more likely to be the correct answer.

A few hints follow on how to make your best guess. These are only hints and will not work every single time. It is always better to use what you know

and select the best answer based on the passage. Use these hints if your only option is making a random guess.

Look for Similar Answers

If you find that two of the answer choices are almost exactly the same, with the exception of a few words, eliminate the other answers and select between these two.

Also Look for Opposite Answers

You may notice that two of the answer choices are opposites.

Which is true about the duck-billed platypus?
a. It lays eggs.
b. It is a bird.
c. It does not lay eggs.
d. It is a vegetarian.

Notice that choices **a** and **c** are opposites, and obviously, both cannot be correct. So, you can automatically eliminate at least one of these answers. In this case, choice **a** happens to be correct. However, keep in mind that in another question, it is possible that both of the opposite answers could be wrong.

Get Rid of Extremes

Sometimes one answer may seem very different from the rest. In this case, eliminate the extreme answer.

Where did the story take place?
a. Alabama
b. Florida
c. Georgia
d. Paraguay

The answer choices here include three southern states and a foreign country. Paraguay seems a little extreme among the other choices in the list. If you are going to try to eliminate an answer so that you can make your best guess, Paraguay might be the most logical choice to eliminate.

Look for Grammatical Hints

Some questions may require you to choose the answer choice that correctly completes a sentence. Look for any choices that do not fit grammatically and eliminate these. For example, if the beginning of the sentence is written in past tense and an answer choice is in present tense, there's a good chance that the answer is incorrect.

If you are asked to choose a missing word or to identify a word with the same meaning, eliminate any choices that are a different part of speech.

The attorney was late for the meeting and asked us to brief her quickly on what had taken place so far.

What best tells the meaning of *brief* in the sentence?
a. concise without detail
b. to summarize in writing
c. a synopsis of a document
d. to give necessary information

In the sentence, *brief* is a verb, so the correct answer will also be a verb. Choice **a** is an adjective, and choice **c** is a noun. These can be eliminated, leaving only answers **b** and **d**, which are both verbs. In this case, **d** is the best choice.

Keeping Track of Time

Remember that this is a timed test. Being aware of how much time has passed and how much time remains can make a tremendous difference in your overall performance.

Wear a Watch

Be sure to wear a watch on the day of the test. Check the time as the test begins and figure out the time at which the test will end. The test administrator will probably update you on how much time remains throughout the test. However, it's a good idea to be able to check for yourself.

Don't Rush

Remember the old saying "Slow and steady wins the race"? Yes, there is a time limit. Yes, you need to pace yourself. However, if you rush, you'll be more likely to make mistakes. Work quickly, but most important, work carefully.

It's better to answer some of the questions and get them right than to answer most of the questions and get them wrong.

Keep an eye on your watch, but keep your focus on doing your best.

TIP

Most people who have not passed the GED® test actually had the knowledge needed to pass. So what was the problem? They ran out of time. Don't let this happen to you! Pace yourself, monitor the time, and keep moving.

Use Your Time Wisely

Don't spend too much time trying to select a single answer. If a question has you stumped, take your best guess and move on. You can always come back later if you have extra time at the end. Wasting time on one tricky question can prevent you from having time to answer another that you might think is a breeze.

TIP

Sometimes, if you skip a tough question and come back to it later, you will find it easier to answer the second time around. Information and clues in other questions may help you figure out the best answer.

Wrap Things Up at the End

You already know the importance of keeping an eye on the time. If you find that there are only a couple of minutes left and you have not yet finished the test, start guessing. Any answer that is left blank will automatically be marked wrong. Go ahead and take a stab at any remaining questions; quickly get an answer marked for every test item. At this point, what have you got to lose? You may or may not get them right, but at least you tried, and as previously noted, there is no guessing penalty.

Tips for Nonfiction Passages

The purpose of the nonfiction passages on the test may be to entertain, inform, or persuade readers. The testing standards of the GED® Reasoning through Language Arts test place a particular emphasis on the understanding and analysis of arguments and evidence, so expect passages that focus on presenting a viewpoint or position on an issue. Regardless of their purpose, these passages are based on actual people, topics, or events and will offer information, facts, and details about the topic.

Notice Details

Watch for details such as statistics, dates, names, events, section headings, and key words that are included in the passage. You may see these again when you get to the questions. However, do not select an answer choice simply because it matches something from the passage; many incorrect answer choices are also taken from the text. This is to ensure that you are understanding the passage and not just skimming for a correct answer.

Pay Attention to Descriptive Language

Descriptive language can offer clues about an author's views on a topic. For example, if an author describes a car as a "beast," that author probably feels that the vehicle is very big or powerful. After you find the main idea, begin looking for language, facts, and details that reveal or support the author's point of view.

Look for Evidence

Keep in mind that each paragraph of a nonfiction passage will have a main idea. The rest of the paragraph will include details to support the main idea. As you read, search for this evidence. Facts, examples, descriptions, and other information that helps explain the main idea are essential to understanding the text and will probably be the subject of at least some of the questions.

Draw Your Own Conclusions

Some types of nonfiction passages will include opinions on a particular topic. In some cases, you will be given two passages that offer different views on the same topic. Pay special attention to the evidence and reasons presented to support the view presented in each passage. Then, draw your own conclusions regarding the author's ability to present and support that opinion. For the extended response item on the test, reaching your own conclusions and expanding on the evidence and views presented in the passages is critical if you want to score well.

Tips for Fiction Passages

Prose fiction passages involve imaginary people and events. While you may see prose fiction passages that contain arguments and evidence to support a viewpoint or conclusion, the author's main intent for prose fiction is generally to entertain. These passages are more likely to focus on tone, style, setting, point of view, and making inferences about the characters and the world.

Make Inferences

Often in prose fiction passages, the author intentionally leaves out some information. This requires readers to make inferences about the plot, characters, or setting. Use the information that is implied to "fill in the blanks" and create your own complete mental picture. For example, you can infer what type of person a character is by paying attention to what other characters say or think about him. You can put together information about the sights, sounds, and smells described in a story to infer the setting.

> *As Maxwell stepped outside, he noticed the sounds of the cows mooing in the distance and could make out the silhouette of the barn on the opposite side of the field. This was nothing like the city he was used to.*

What is the setting of the story?
a. a barn
b. a big city
c. a farm
d. a zoo

The writer mentions a city, but this is not the setting. Because we know that Maxwell hears cows and can see a barn on the other side of the field, we can infer that he is on a farm (choice **c**). If the barn were the setting, he would be in it or near it; it would not be in the distance.

Notice Names

Pay close attention to the names of people and places, as well as to dates and key words. These are often important to remember if you are going to accurately understand the story.

Pay Attention to Details

Details can help you determine many things about a story. This information is invaluable when answering questions about plot, conflicts, mood, point of view, and theme. If you get to a question about one of these and are unsure of the answer, look back in the passage and see what insight the details can offer.

Preparing for the Test

Like so many things, the key to doing well on the GED® test is preparation. You're already on the right track by reading these chapters. A few other tips to help you prepare are discussed in this section.

Practice, Practice, Practice

Taking a practice test, such as the ones in this book, is a terrific way to be sure you are ready. These practice tests help you in several ways:

- You will know what types of questions to expect.
- You will become comfortable with the format of the test.
- You will learn about your own strengths and weaknesses.
- You will be aware of what you need to study.

As you take the practice tests, pay attention to the types of questions you get right and those that are more challenging. For example, you may find that the questions about main ideas are really easy. That's great! You might also find that you miss a lot of the questions that deal with themes. No problem. Now you know what skills to study.

Create Opportunities for Even More Practice

You probably read different types of passages all the time, either in magazines or newspapers, in novels, or on the Internet. As you read, think about the types of questions you will find on the GED® test. Then, ask yourself questions about your reading material. For example, you might ask yourself:

- What is the main idea of the passage I just read?
- What details support the main idea?
- What were the conflict and resolution in this story?
- What context clues helped me determine the meanings of unfamiliar words?
- What is the theme (or tone or mood) of the passage?

Another idea is to work with a friend and write questions for each other based on passages you select. You could also summarize passages, underline key words, circle the main idea of each paragraph, and highlight supporting details.

Know Yourself

Figure out what works best for you. For example, not everyone benefits from reading the questions before reading the passage. Some people may find it helpful to scan a passage for the main idea before reading; others may not. Try different strategies as you work through the practice questions and pay attention to which strategies you find most comfortable and most beneficial.

Be Ready the Day Before the Test

Being ready mentally and physically can help you do your best on the test. Here are some suggestions:

- Start studying and preparing in advance; don't plan on cramming for the test in the few days before you are scheduled to take it.
- The day before the test, take a break and relax. Go for a walk, call a friend, or see a movie. Don't stay up late to study.
- Have anything you want to take with you ready ahead of time. Set out your pencils, sweater, watch, or anything else that you need to take to the test location in the morning.
- Make sure you get plenty of sleep the night before the test. If you're concerned that you won't be able to fall asleep, get up extra early the morning before the test. That way, you'll be ready for bed early that evening.

The Big Day

You've studied, you're well rested, and now you're ready to take the GED® Reasoning through Language Arts exam! Now that test day is here, make the most of it.

Get Off to a Good Start

First, set your alarm early enough so that you won't have to rush. Not only will you feel more relaxed and have time to get settled before the test starts, but you also might not be allowed to enter the testing center if you are late. Make sure that being on time is one thing you won't have to worry about.

Then, be sure to eat a well-balanced breakfast. You need to keep your energy up, and you certainly don't want to be distracted by the sound of your stomach growling. If today is going to be a long day of testing, bring a bottle of water, a piece of fruit, or some trail mix to snack on between sessions.

Also, dress in comfortable, layered clothes and bring a sweater. Feeling like your shoes are too tight or being too hot or too cold can be distractions. Do everything you can to be sure you feel great and are on top of your game today!

Keep Your Cool

You've studied, you've practiced, and now you're ready. Don't let your nerves get the best of you. Getting worked up will not help you get your highest possible score. In the overall scheme of things, the GED® test is just a test. If things don't go as well as you'd hoped today, consider this a practice run. You have three chances in a calendar year to pass the test. Try to stay calm and focus on doing your best.

Carefully Read the Directions

If you are unsure about the directions or what exactly you are supposed to do, be sure to ask the test administrator before you begin the test. He or she cannot help you with specific test questions or vocabulary, but you may be able to get the information you need to clarify the test's instructions.

Quiz

Directions: Choose the *one best answer* to each question.

Questions 1 through 4 refer to the following passage:

Which Pieces of Art Are the Artist's Best Work?

Local up-and-coming artist Melanie O'Keefe debuted a number of pieces from her collection at the Laurel Oaks Fine Art Museum recently. Attendance at the showing
(5) exceeded expectations and brought a number of renowned art critics to the downtown area. Members of the museum's board of directors were impressed by O'Keefe's display as well as excited about the
(10) attention the show brought to the museum itself.

The most prominent piece in the collection, "Springtime Rain," will remain on display for approximately one year. This
(15) piece depicts two barefoot young children walking through a field of brightly colored wildflowers during a spring rain shower. The artist's use of light creates a warm effect through the mostly overcast sky and gives a
(20) cheerful feeling to the piece, while the softening of each line nearly creates the effect of looking out of a rain-streaked windowpane. Her attention to detail in each brushstroke lends a professional quality to
(25) the work of a relative newcomer in the field.

O'Keefe's signature watercolor piece, "Winter in the City," depicts a cityscape of the early years of our own town, including only a few early model vehicles and several
(30) residents wrapped in heavy coats and scarves, walking along the brick roads. The artist's use of texture and shadow allows museum

(35) visitors to feel the chill in the air and hear the sounds of the wind whistling between the buildings. The use of various shades of grays and blues adds to the depth of the piece while helping to create the feelings of a winter day. The subtle use of white light to illuminate the streetlamps

(40) nearly causes them to pop off the canvas.

The charcoal drawings in the collection drew an impressive amount of attention from visitors, although these works do not display the same quality as her works done

(45) in other mediums. The overall images are pleasant to view but portray an amateur feel. "Cottage on the Shore" was undoubtedly the most memorable piece created in this portion of the show; however, it was the

(50) subject matter rather than the talent of the artist that will remain in the viewers' minds. It is apparent that these are the earliest pieces O'Keefe created.

1. Based on the passage, all the following statements are true about Melanie O'Keefe EXCEPT which one?
   a. She is a relatively new artist.
   b. Painting is her favorite form of art.
   c. Her work was displayed in the museum.
   d. The names of two of her pieces mention seasons.

2. Which is true about the writer of the commentary?
   a. The writer enjoys art exhibitions by local artists the best.
   b. The writer never likes artwork that includes the use of charcoal.
   c. The writer always prefers watercolor paintings to other art forms.
   d. The writer felt the charcoal drawings were the weakest in the collection.

3. What can be concluded about the artist and her work?
   a. The artist included an impressive use of light in all the pieces in the display.
   b. The artist's use of light is one of the prominent aspects of some of her artwork.
   c. The artist's use of light is better in "Winter in the City" than in "Springtime Rain."
   d. The artist's use of light is better in "Springtime Rain" than in "Winter in the City."

4. Which statement can be inferred about the artwork in the exhibit?
   a. "Springtime Rain" was created using paint.
   b. "Winter in the City" was the most recent piece on display.
   c. "Cottage on the Shore" showed use of texture and shadow.
   d. "Springtime Rain" and "Winter in the City" were both watercolors.

Answers

1. b. Notice that the question includes the word *except*. The answer choices include three statements that are true, based on the passage, and one that is not. While several of the pieces in the exhibit were paintings, nothing in the passage states that this is her favorite form of art. This question is an example of why it is crucial that test takers carefully read every word; had someone overlooked the word *except*, he or she might have been looking for a statement that was true rather than the one statement that was not true.

2. d. Choice **d** is the only one supported by the information in the passage. Choices **b** and **c** might be tempting because the statements contain some truth in regard to this particular art show; the writer does prefer these paintings to the charcoal drawings. However, remember what you read about answers that are absolutes. These choices include the words *never* and *always*. If you needed to eliminate incorrect answer choices, these would be a good place to start. The passage does not suggest that the writer always likes one form of art and never likes another. Remember, very few things *always* or *never* occur.

3. b. The artist's use of light is mentioned in the reviews of both "Springtime Rain" and "Winter in the City," implying that this is one of the most noticeable or important aspects of these pieces. Suppose you were unsure of which answer choice was correct. Which could be eliminated to help you make a strong guess? Notice that choice **a** includes the word *all*. This word is an absolute that must be carefully considered before selecting this answer. If you needed to get rid of one option, this might be a good one to eliminate. Then, notice that choices **c** and **d** are opposites. Obviously one, if not both, of these can be eliminated. In this case, nothing in the passage indicates that the use of light is better in one piece than it is in the other, so both can be eliminated.

4. a. Here's an example of why readers need to notice details. Without paying attention to the name of each piece of artwork, it would be difficult to know which statements are true about the artist's displays. The passage never directly states that "Springtime Rain" is a painting, but the attention to detail in each brushstroke is mentioned. Because brushstrokes are used in painting, readers can infer that this piece is a painting. While the writer does mention that the charcoal drawings are the artist's earliest works, he or she does not tell which work is the most recent. The use of texture and shadow, watercolors, and professionalism are mentioned in the passage, but not regarding the pieces named in choices **c** and **d**.

In this chapter, you learned a number of tips that will help you do your best on the GED® Reasoning through Language Arts test:

1. Before you begin reading a passage, be sure to pay attention to the purpose question that precedes the passage as well as the comprehension questions that follow it.

2. Scan the passage first, then read it carefully, noticing important details and mentally organizing the information. Remember to read the information in brackets, the visual aids, and the captions as well.

3. After you read the passage completely, thoroughly read each question, paying close attention to any information stated within the question itself.

4. Try to answer each question before you actually read the answer choices. Then, read each choice carefully, paying close attention to every word, before selecting the best answer based on the passage.

5. After selecting an answer, reread the question to make sure your answer choice is the best fit.

6. Answer every single question, even if it means you have to guess.

7. If you are unsure of which answer to choose, look for options that are similar or are opposites, contain extremes, or have grammatical hints. Then, eliminate as many choices as possible before taking your best guess. Remember, the more options you eliminate, the better your chance of choosing the correct response.

8. Because the GED® test is timed, it is essential that you are aware of the time. Wear a watch, pace yourself, and don't spend too much time on any one question. If you see that time is running out, quickly select an answer for each of the remaining questions.

9. As you read nonfiction passages, look for evidence that supports the main idea of the passage. Be sure to pay close attention to details, names, dates, statistics, and descriptive language that can enhance your comprehension of the material and help you draw your own conclusions about the topic.

10. When reading fiction passages, be sure to pay attention to details, such as the names of characters or places, and use the ideas that are included in the passage to infer information that the author has not included.

11. Practicing for the test can help you feel prepared, show you important information about your own strengths and weaknesses, and make you aware of the strategies that work best for you.

12. Take a break the day before the test. Don't study too much that day, and be sure to get a good night's sleep.

13. Get up early and have a good breakfast on the morning of the test. Wear comfortable clothes and dress in layers in case the testing center is too warm or too cool for your liking.

14. Read the test directions carefully and ask questions if you need to.

7 ▶ WRITING AN EFFECTIVE ESSAY

CHAPTER SUMMARY

In this chapter, you'll learn how to recognize the parts of an effective essay. You'll also learn how to use the basic steps of the writing process to plan and draft an effective essay in response to a given prompt.

About the GED® Test Extended Response Question

The GED® Reasoning through Language Arts test features one extended response item that requires you to write a short essay in response to a reading passage or pair of passages. These reading passages are between 550 and 650 words, and will focus on presenting arguments or viewpoints along with supporting evidence. Your job will be to analyze these arguments and evidence, incorporating your own knowledge and views while still focusing mainly on the author and his or her intent. Your extended response should always include evidence presented within the passage itself as the main basis for your arguments. You should also analyze or evaluate the validity of the evidence presented in the passage. Note that this test item is not about choosing the "right" or "wrong" side of an issue. It is intended to test your ability to understand, analyze, and evaluate arguments.

Analyzing the Prompt

The prompt is the text that appears after the reading passage(s) and explains what your extended response should cover. While it may not seem significant, the **prompt** is your key to figuring out the main idea for your extended response. The prompt will tell you exactly what you should write about. For example, take a look at this prompt:

> *In your response, develop an argument about how the author's position reflects the idea of "the common good" in American society.*

Even without reading the passage(s), you already know the topic of your response: "the common good" in American society, and how it is reflected in the reading passage. It will still be up to you to analyze the author's arguments, reasoning, and evidence and relate those to the topic mentioned in the prompt.

It is important to analyze the prompt prior to thinking in detail about your response. If, for example, the reading passage(s) that accompanied the sample prompt focused mainly on Social Security, you might think that the response should also focus mainly on Social Security. However, Social Security is not mentioned in the prompt. This is because you are being asked to place the author's position on Social Security into a larger context, covering the broad topic of "the common good" in American society. Remember that your extended response will not be about summarizing the reading passage(s); it will be about analyzing the information and details presented in the passage(s) to reach your own conclusions.

What's in an Essay

An **essay** is a short piece of nonfiction writing that presents the writer's point of view on a particular subject. Remember, *short* is a relative term; in this case, it basically means *shorter than a book*. An essay can actually be as short as a paragraph or two, or as long as 50 pages. On the GED® test, you'll want to shoot for a four or five paragraph essay.

Every essay has three main parts: an **introduction**, a **body**, and a **conclusion**, also known as a **beginning**, **middle**, and **end**. In a five-paragraph essay, the first paragraph is the introduction, the last paragraph is the conclusion, and the three paragraphs in the middle are the body.

The Introduction

The *introduction* is the first paragraph in an essay. In a five-paragraph essay such as the one you'll be writing for the GED® test, the introduction is usually about three or four sentences long. It has three main purposes:

- state the main idea of the essay
- catch the reader's attention
- set the tone for the rest of the essay

Stating the Main Idea

A **main idea** is the main thing the writer wants the reader to know. The main idea of a paragraph is stated in the **topic sentence**, and the topic sentence is often the first sentence of the paragraph. Like a paragraph, an essay has a main idea. It is stated in a single sentence called the **thesis statement**, which is generally the last sentence of the introduction.

On the GED® test, your thesis statement should be a clear, concise answer to the prompt. For example, a possible thesis sentence for a sample prompt asking what you would choose if you could relive one day of your life might be as follows:

> *If I could do one thing in my life again, I would relive my wedding day.*

This is a good thesis statement because it clearly answers the question in the prompt. It also presents the main idea of the essay without trying to tell the reader too much at once.

Catching the Reader's Attention

In addition to containing the thesis statement, a good introduction starts off with a couple of sentences that catch the reader's attention. Obviously, the content of these sentences will vary widely depending on your thesis statement. A possible introduction based on the sample thesis statement provided might look something like this:

What if you could live one day of your life over again? Some people might choose to relive a day in order to change something about their lives. Others might simply want a second chance to enjoy a great experience. If I could do one thing in my life again, I would relive my wedding day.

As you can see, the three sentences at the beginning of the paragraph lead into the thesis statement in a relatively engaging way. It might not be *Harry Potter*, but it's definitely better than the following approach:

This is my paper about the thing I would like to do over again in my life. I would like to live my wedding day over again.

The people who grade GED® test extended responses read dozens, perhaps even hundreds of essays written from the same prompt. An essay with a clear, creative introduction will almost certainly earn a higher score than an introduction that merely states what the essay is supposed to be about.

Setting the Tone for the Essay

Finally, a good introduction sets the tone for the rest of the essay. **Tone** refers to the attitude the writer takes toward the subject and the reader. For example, your tone might be formal, informal, humorous, ironic, aggressive, or apologetic. The tone you choose depends to some extent on your purpose for writing. For example, if your purpose is to amuse the reader, your tone will be humorous.

On the GED® test, it is a good idea to use a formal tone. That means using standard English vocabulary and grammar, rather than casual slang such as you might use with a friend. You should strive to use complete sentences with correct grammar and punctuation, and to keep contractions (words like *can't*, *don't*, and *won't*) to a minimum. Using a formal tone in your writing shows respect for your readers while proving that you are able to write correctly.

To better understand the difference between formal and informal tone, take a look at the following examples. The first example is written using an informal tone. The second uses a formal tone. In both examples the thesis statement is bold so that you can easily locate it.

Example 1: *You know, living your life over again would be like a dream. I guess some people would want to go back and try to change something they messed up the first time, and some people would probably just want to relive a day when they did something really cool.* **I would totally do my wedding day again.**

Example 2: *What if you could live one day of your life over again? Some people might choose to relive a day in order to change something about their lives. Others might simply want a second chance to enjoy a great experience.* **If I could do one thing in my life again, I would relive my wedding day.**

While the first example may be a more accurate representation of how people speak, it is not an acceptable way to write an academic essay. The second example uses a tone that is appropriate to academic writing. You will be expected to write using a similar tone on the GED® test.

Notice that in both introductions the thesis statement is the last sentence of the paragraph. You should strive to structure your introductions in the same way. Just as business people generally chat for a few minutes before *getting down to business,* a good writer strives to get the reader's attention before stating the essay's main idea.

Now you try it. Using the space below, draft and write *an introduction only* in response to the following prompt:

What is your favorite thing? Whether it is a gift you were given during your childhood or something you saved up for years for and bought, you probably have something that is special to you. Write about this special object and why it is important to you.

Introduction:

_____

_____

_____

_____

_____

The Body

The *body* is the part of the essay where you develop and defend your argument. Like the essay itself, the body can range from a single paragraph to many pages in length. For the purposes of the GED® test, however, the body of your essay should be two or three paragraphs long.

You have learned that each paragraph must have a topic sentence stating the main idea of the paragraph. As previously mentioned, it's a good idea to make the topic sentence the first sentence of the paragraph so that your reader knows right away what the paragraph is going to be about.

The following paragraph is an example of a body paragraph that might follow the sample introduction on reliving one's wedding day:

Reliving my wedding day would give me the opportunity to see my family together again. It was the only day of my life when my mom's and my dad's families came together to celebrate in one place. Furthermore, my

wedding day was the last time I saw my grandfather because he passed away a few weeks later.

The first sentence is the topic sentence and states the main idea of the paragraph—that reliving the wedding day would allow the writer to see his or her family together again. The other sentences support the main idea by providing examples of how the family was united that day. As a whole, the paragraph develops the main idea of the essay, which is that the writer would like to experience his or her wedding day again.

It's your turn. Using the space provided, write a thesis and body paragraph that explores the following prompt.

What is your favorite thing? Whether it is a gift you were given during your childhood or something you saved up for years for and bought, you probably have something that is special to you. Write about this special object and why it is important to you.

Your thesis:

_____

_____

Body paragraph:

_____

_____

_____

_____

_____

The Conclusion

The *conclusion* is the final paragraph of the essay. A good conclusion should accomplish the following things:

1. restate the main idea
2. give the reader a sense of closure

Restating the Main Idea

The purpose of restating the main idea in the conclusion is twofold; first, it reminds the reader of the most important thing you want him or her to remember. Second, it gives the essay a more unified feeling.

Restating the main idea, however, doesn't necessarily mean writing the exact same thing or simply switching the words around. You can be more creative this time around, including adding some extra information or restating your ideas in a new and interesting way. Here's one way to restate the thesis statement we've been working with throughout this chapter:

Original thesis:

If I could do one thing in my life again, I would relive my wedding day.

Restated:

Though I will never have the chance, I would love to be able to experience my wedding day again.

In this example, the main idea is given in both sentences, but in the second one it includes something more: the idea that reliving any moment of one's life is impossible. It adds a sense of regret to the essay that can leave the reader feeling pleasantly wistful.

Now it's your turn to write. Using the following lines, rewrite the thesis statement you wrote in the previous example as it would appear in the conclusion of your essay.

Original thesis:

_____

_____

Restated thesis:

_____

_____

Giving the Reader a Sense of Closure

To give readers a sense of closure means to make them feel satisfied with how the essay ends. It's difficult to say specifically what to do so that people come away with this feeling. It's fairly easy, however, to say what _not_ to do. To ensure that readers feel a sense of closure at the end of your essay,

- don't introduce completely new ideas.
- don't only refer to narrow, specific examples.
- don't end your essay with a question.

An example of an effective conclusion for the topic of reliving some moment of your life would be:

Beautiful weather, a fairytale setting, my happy family; for one day of my life, everything was perfect. Although I know I will never have the chance, I would love to experience my wedding day again.

As you can see, the conclusion doesn't have to be long and involved. It just needs to be a long enough to tie the essay together and leave the reader feeling satisfied. Although conclusions can be difficult to write well, it becomes easier with practice.

Using the following space, write a conclusion for the essay you've been working on in the previous examples. Include the restated thesis you wrote in the last exercise.

Original thesis:

_____

_____

Restated thesis:

_____

_____

Conclusion:

_____

_____

_____

_____

_____

How to Write a Powerful Essay

An *effective* essay is one that clearly and completely accomplishes its purpose. There are many possible purposes for an essay: to inform, to persuade, to entertain, to compare, to prove, or to disprove. The purpose of your essay on the GED® test will most likely be either to inform the reader regarding your opinion of an issue or to persuade the reader to agree with your point of view on an issue.

Planning

Writing an effective essay requires planning, something that new writers are often reluctant to do. Why? Many students are impatient and just want to get the job over with. Others worry that taking the time to plan out their essay will cause them to run out of time to write.

However, planning what you are going to write beforehand should make the writing process much smoother and easier. It will also help you come up with ideas for what to write, organize your ideas effectively, and express your ideas clearly once you start writing. Most of the writing you did in the last section of this chapter was much like planning; in this section, you will learn how to plan more.

There are three main steps to successfully planning an essay:

1. come up with a thesis statement
2. brainstorm ideas related to your thesis statement
3. organize your ideas into an outline

The following subsections describe each step in detail.

Coming Up with a Thesis Statement

Many students find it difficult to come up with an effective thesis statement. Often, writing a thesis statement for the GED® test is as simple as answering a question about yourself, a question that may appear in the prompt. Then all you have to do is answer it. For example:

> *What is your favorite thing? Whether it is a gift you were given during your childhood or something you saved up for years for and bought, you probably have something that is special to you. Write about this special object and why it is important to you.*

The question here is *What is your favorite thing?* Your thesis statement should answer that question in a complete sentence.

Sometimes, the prompt provided is in the form of a statement. In this case, there will be a sentence that gives you instructions to *tell*, *describe*, or *explain* something. Simply take the sentence that instructs you to do something and turn it into a question. For example:

> *Many people believe that humans' spirits remain on earth after they die, in the form of ghosts. Explain why you do or do not believe that ghosts exist.*

Notice that the second sentence of the prompt gives you instructions: *Explain why.* Drop the word *explain* and turn the statement into a question: *Do you or do you not believe that ghosts exist?* Again, your thesis statement should answer that question. Let's practice what you've learned so far. Write a thesis statement in response to the following prompt:

> *Embarrassing moments often remain clear in our memories, despite the fact that we would like to forget them. Tell about one of your most embarrassing experiences.*

Thesis statement:

_____

_____

Brainstorming Your Ideas

Brainstorm is simply another way of saying _write down anything you can think of as fast as you possibly can._ The purpose of brainstorming is to help you get all your ideas down on paper so that you can figure out how to organize them later.

So let's say you've come up with the following thesis statement: _If I could do one thing in my life again, I would relive my wedding day._ To brainstorm ideas related to this thesis, you would take out a blank sheet of paper, write your thesis at the top, and then spend about three or four minutes writing down whatever related thoughts come to you, in no particular order. Here is a sample brainstorm on this thesis statement:

- _flowers_
- _beautiful day_
- _perfect temperature_
- _no rain_
- _family together_
- _husband handsome_
- _felt like a princess_
- _beautiful hair_
- _grandmother's dress_
- _mom and dad happy_
- _mom's family and dad's family_
- _no fighting_
- _laughter_
- _great music_

At this point, the brainstorm doesn't look anything like an essay; it just looks like a bunch of ideas. The next thing to do is to sort through the mess by going over each thing you wrote down, circling related ideas, and connecting them by drawing a line between them. This leaves you with a brainstorm that looks like this:

The largest groups in the brainstorm should tell you what the main ideas will be for the body of your essay. In this brainstorm, there are three ideas related to the weather (beautiful day, perfect temperature, no rain), three related to the bride's appearance (felt like a princess, beautiful hair, grandmother's dress), and five ideas related to the family (family together, mom and dad happy, mom's family and dad's family, no fighting, and laughter). That means the two body paragraphs in the essay should have to do with weather, her appearance, and the family.

Now it's your turn to brainstorm. Using the space provided, brainstorm about your favorite object and why it's important to you.

_____

_____

_____

_____

Organizing Your Ideas

The next step in the planning process is to organize your ideas into an essay outline. An **outline** is basically a list of the major elements in your essay: introduction (ending with the thesis statement), topic sentences, support, and conclusion, in the order in which you plan to write them.

Here's a sample outline structure. To create an outline for an essay, all you need to do is fill in the blanks.

Introduction:

_____

_____

_____

_____

_____

Thesis Statement:

_____

_____

Body Paragraph #1—Topic Sentence:

_____

_____

Support #1:

_____

_____

Support #2:

_____

_____

Support #3:

_____

_____

Body Paragraph #2—Topic Sentence:

_____

_____

_____

_____

_____

_____

Support #1:

_____

_____

Support #2:

_____

_____

Support #3:

_____

_____

Body Paragraph #3—Topic Sentence:

_____

_____

_____

_____

_____

_____

Support #1:

_____

_____

Support #2:

_____

_____

Support #3:

_____

_____

Conclusion:

_____

_____

_____

_____

_____

You should have already written a thesis statement when you started planning, so that part's done. The next thing to do is to write the main ideas for your body paragraphs as topic sentences. Remember, a topic sentence is a complete sentence that states the main idea of the paragraph.

In the example we've been using, the main ideas focus on weather and family. To turn these ideas into topic sentences, you need to answer the question, *What about them?* What about the weather? Was it terrible? Was it boring? No, according to the notes in the brainstorm, the weather on the writer's wedding day was perfect. So a topic sentence on that main idea could simply state, *The weather was perfect on my wedding day.* It could also be more creative, *On my wedding day the weather was more beautiful than I would have ever imagined.*

Let's say the writer has come up with the following three topic sentences:

Topic sentence #1:
The weather was perfect on my wedding day.

Topic sentence #2:
I felt like a princess on my wedding day.

Topic sentence #3:
The best thing about my wedding day was seeing my family together.

These three sentences should be added to the outline. The order they go in depends on the writer's purpose, but on the GED® test, it's a good idea to go with order of importance. Therefore, whichever idea is least important should come first, followed by the next important, and finally the most important.

The next step is filling in the support. **Supporting sentences** provide examples and help to explain the main idea. Flip back to the brainstorm for a minute and take a look at all the ideas that are related to weather. Some of those ideas can be used as support.

Body Paragraph #1—Topic Sentence:
The weather was perfect on my wedding day.

Support #1:
perfect temperature

Support #2:
no rain

You don't have to have exactly three supporting sentences for each topic sentence; you can write more or fewer as the situation requires. It's a good idea, however, to shoot for at least two. If you have fewer than two supporting sentences, there's a good chance that you haven't fully explored the main idea.

Like topic sentences, supporting sentences should be organized. You can put them in order from least to most important, chronological order, or ordered by cause and effect.

Also note that for the purposes of an outline, it's not necessary to write out the support in complete sentences. You will expand the notes into complete sentences during the writing process.

SAVE TIME

Save time during the planning process by writing short phrases, rather than complete sentences, for your essay support. You'll have time to flesh things out when you start writing.

The final step in writing the outline is to draft your conclusion. Remember, a good conclusion should restate the thesis statement and give the reader a sense of closure.

Essay Outline

A complete essay outline will look something like this:

Introduction:
What if you could live one day of your life over again? Some people might choose to relive a day to change something about their lives. Others might simply want a second chance to enjoy a great experience.

Thesis statement:
As for me, if I could do one thing in my life again, I would relive my wedding day.

Body Paragraph #1 (Topic Sentence):
The weather was perfect on my wedding day.

Support #1:
perfect temperature

Support #2:
no rain

Body Paragraph #2 (Topic Sentence):
I felt like a princess that day.

Support #1:
beautiful hair

Support #2:
holding flowers

Support #3:
wearing my grandmother's dress

Body Paragraph #3 (Topic Sentence):
The best thing about my wedding day was seeing my family happy together.

Support #1:
mom's and dad's family there

Support #2:
no fighting

Support #3:
everyone laughing

Conclusion:
Beautiful weather, a fairytale setting, my happy family; for one day of my life, everything was perfect. Though I know I will never have the chance, I would love to experience my wedding day again.

That's it for planning. Now you know what your essay is going to be about, what the topic sentences of your body paragraphs are going to be, and what support you're going to use to back them up. You're now ready to move on to the next step: writing the essay.

Using the following outline form as a guide, create an outline for the essay topic you've been working on about your favorite object.

Introduction:

_____

_____

_____

_____

Thesis Statement:

_____

_____

Body Paragraph #1—Topic Sentence:

_____

_____

_____

_____

Support #1:

_____

_____

Support #2:

_____

_____

Support #3:

_____

_____

Body Paragraph #2—Topic Sentence:

_____

_____

_____

_____

Support #1:

_____

_____

Support #2:

_____

_____

Support #3:

_____

_____

Body Paragraph #3—Topic Sentence:

_____

_____

_____

_____

Support #1:

_____

_____

Support #2:

_____

_____

Support #3:

_____

_____

Conclusion:

_____

_____

_____

_____

Writing

Once you've thoroughly planned your essay, writing it should be a relatively simple process of expanding on what you've already written in your outline. As mentioned in previous sections, you'll want to begin your introduction with a few sentences to catch the reader's attention and lead into the thesis statement. Each body paragraph will start with the topic sentence you've already written and continue with the support you've noted to explain and develop the main idea. Finally, the conclusion will bring the essay to an end, restating the thesis and giving the reader a sense of closure.

A sample essay based on the outline in the previous section might look like this:

What if you could live one day of your life over again? Some people might choose to relive a day to change something about their lives. Others might simply want a second chance to enjoy a great experience. As for me, if I could do one thing in my life again, I would relive my wedding day.

The weather was perfect on my wedding day. Although it was supposed to rain that day, it didn't. The sun was shining, and the temperature was perfect. I could tell from the start that it was going to be a great day.

I felt like a princess that day. My hair was styled beautifully. As I walked down the aisle, I carried a bouquet of daisies, just as I had always imagined princesses doing as a little girl. I was even wearing my grandmother's wedding dress, which had a long, old-fashioned train, just as I imagine royalty must wear.

The best thing about my wedding day was seeing my family happy together. My parents are divorced, but both my mom and my dad's families came to the wedding. For the first time in my life, they didn't fight. They were all laughing together and having a good time.

Beautiful weather, a fairytale setting, my happy family; for one day of my life, everything was perfect. Though I know I will never have the chance, I would love to experience my wedding day again.

Now it's your turn. Write an essay on your favorite object, using all the tools and strategies covered thus far. The prompt is reprinted below for your convenience.

What is your favorite thing? Whether it is a gift you were given during your childhood or something you saved up for years for and bought, you probably have something that is special to you. Write about this special object and why it is important to you.

Revising an Essay

Good planning can save you a lot of time, both in writing and in revising your essay. Ideally, you should not have to make any major revisions like adding sentences or moving paragraphs around. However, it is a good idea to take the last few minutes before your time is up to read over your essay and check for proper grammar, punctuation, and word choice. Here are a few things to look out for:

- **Capitalization.** Make sure the first word of every sentence and all proper nouns are capitalized.
- **Punctuation.** Make sure you've ended each sentence with a period or a question mark, as appropriate. Also check to see that you haven't thrown in any unnecessary punctuation, like commas or apostrophes.
- **Spelling.** Double-check homonyms like *to/too*, *its/it's*, *your/you're*, and *there/their/they're*. It's easy to make mistakes with them when you're in a hurry.
- **Repetition.** If you see a word, a phrase, or an idea that has been repeated, draw a single line through the second usage.
- **Unrelated information.** If you come across a sentence that has nothing to do with the rest of your essay, draw a line through it.
- **Clarity.** If something in your essay doesn't make sense to you, it probably won't make sense to anyone else, either. Take a moment to figure out what you were trying to say and rewrite it.

If you've spent enough time in the planning phase and followed your outline well, you should need no more than five minutes to complete your revisions. When time is up, you should feel confident that you are handing in a complete and well-written essay.

How Your Essay Is Scored

The extended response essay on the GED® Reasoning through Language Arts test is scored in three different categories. In each category, you can receive up to 2 points, for a total of 6 points maximum. This score is then doubled and included in your overall point score for the test.

The categories in which your extended response will be scored are:

- creation of arguments and use of evidence
- development of ideas and organizational structure
- clarity and command of standard English conventions

Essentially, the first category focuses on the ideas you present in your essay. The second category focuses on the way in which you present those ideas. The third category focuses on your ability to express those ideas in writing by following rules of spelling, grammar, and basic mechanics and conventions of the language.

Creation of Arguments and Use of Evidence

In this category, you will be evaluated on several different aspects related to the ideas you present. First, the ideas should be relevant to the extended response prompt. You may have a beautifully crafted argument, but if it does not focus on the topic mentioned in the prompt, you will not receive a top score.

Second, your argument or position must be supported by information from the source text(s). Use the information and details from the reading passage(s) to support your claims. However, do not include overly long quotes taken directly from the reading passage(s), since this will look like you are trying to fill space or simply copy what was already stated. Also, make sure that the specific details you cite are relevant to the argument you are making. If you include irrelevant details that do not support your argument, you may receive a lower score.

Third, your extended response essay should evaluate the claims or positions made in the reading passage(s). In other words, you should indicate in your response the validity of the authors' positions by determining whether their arguments are sound or flawed, and provide reasons and evidence to back up your evaluation. Simply stating "the author's reasoning was valid" will not be enough to achieve a top score.

Development of Ideas and Organizational Structure

For this category, the most important element is how your ideas are structured and presented. This means that your essay should flow logically when presenting the steps of an argument; do not jump around in an attempt to cram in as many different ideas as you can think of. The best essays will feature several ideas taken from the main reading passage(s), but those ideas will be expanded and elaborated on in ways that reflect the central idea of your essay. The ideas should also be arranged in a logical progression that builds toward the broadest or most significant points at the end.

Your essay will also be evaluated on its organizational structure. Be sure that each paragraph focuses on a single central idea. Also, be sure to use transitions appropriately when moving from one idea or argument to another. Simply listing facts or arguments in a series is not representative of a high-scoring essay.

Another important element in this category is your use of style appropriate to the audience and purpose of the essay. In general, your extended response essay should be written in a formal style with a tone that avoids bias. Note that bias is different from a well-supported argument. Bias includes the use of emotionally charged words; for example, an

essay that refers to unemployed people as "loafers" exhibits bias and an informal writing style inappropriate for the intended audience.

Clarity and Command of Standard English Conventions

This category focuses on your ability to write according to the basic rules of English grammar, spelling, and related mechanics. The variety of your sentence structure will also be evaluated under this category; try to include sentences of various lengths, but do not create awkward sentences just for the sake of adding length. The same basic rules of usage that apply to other writing-related portions of the test also apply here. Double-check for frequently confused or misspelled words, subject-verb agreement, correct use of pronouns, correct use of capitalization, and appropriate use of punctuation. Note that your extended response does not have to be flawless in this category to earn a high score. However, it is always worth it to reread your essay and check over these basic issues.

Sample Extended Response Question

Read the following pair of speech excerpts, consider the prompt, and take a look at the sample essay provided.

Excerpt from President George W. Bush's Speech on Global Climate Change, June 11, 2001

> *Our country, the United States, is the world's largest emitter of manmade greenhouse gases. We account for almost 20 percent of the world's man-made greenhouse emissions. We also account for about one-quarter of the world's economic output. We recognize the responsibility to reduce our emissions. We also recognize the other part of the story—that the rest of the world emits 80 percent of all*

greenhouse gases. And many of those emissions come from developing countries.

This is a challenge that requires a 100 percent effort; ours, and the rest of the world's. The world's second-largest emitter of greenhouse gases is China. Yet, China was entirely exempted from the requirements of the Kyoto Protocol.

India and Germany are among the top emitters. Yet, India was also exempt from Kyoto. These and other developing countries that are experiencing rapid growth face challenges in reducing their emissions without harming their economies. We want to work cooperatively with these countries in their efforts to reduce greenhouse emissions and maintain economic growth.

Kyoto also failed to address two major pollutants that have an impact on warming: black soot and tropospheric ozone. Both are proven health hazards. Reducing both would not only address climate change, but also dramatically improve people's health.

Kyoto is, in many ways, unrealistic. Many countries cannot meet their Kyoto targets. The targets themselves were arbitrary and not based upon science. For America, complying with those mandates would have a negative economic impact, with layoffs of workers and price increases for consumers. And when you evaluate all these flaws, most reasonable people will understand that it's not sound public policy.

Excerpt from President Barack Obama's speech on climate change at Georgetown University, June 25, 2013

In my State of the Union address, I urged Congress to come up with a bipartisan, market-based solution to climate change, like the one that Republican and Democratic senators worked on together a few years ago. And I still want to see that happen. I'm willing to work with anyone to make that happen.

But this is a challenge that does not pause for partisan gridlock. It demands our attention now. And this is my plan to meet it—a plan to cut carbon pollution; a plan to protect our country from the impacts of climate change; and a plan to lead the world in a coordinated assault on a changing climate. . . .

Now, what you'll hear from the special interests and their allies in Congress is that this will kill jobs and crush the economy, and basically end American free enterprise as we know it. And the reason I know you'll hear those things is because that's what they said every time America sets clear rules and better standards for our air and our water and our children's health. And every time, they've been wrong.

For example, in 1970, when we decided through the Clean Air Act to do something about the smog that was choking our cities— and, by the way, most young people here aren't old enough to remember what it was like, but when I was going to school in 1979–1980 in Los Angeles, there were days where folks couldn't go outside. And the sunsets were spectacular because of all the pollution in the air.

But at the time when we passed the Clean Air Act to try to get rid of some of this smog, some of the same doomsayers were saying new pollution standards will decimate the auto industry. Guess what—it didn't happen. Our air got cleaner.

In 1990, when we decided to do something about acid rain, they said our electricity bills would go up, the lights would go off, businesses around the country would suffer—I quote—"a quiet death." None of it happened, except we cut acid rain dramatically.

See, the problem with all these tired excuses for inaction is that it suggests a fundamental lack of faith in American business and American ingenuity. These critics seem to think that when we ask our businesses to innovate and reduce pollution and lead, they can't or they won't do it. They'll just kind of give up and quit. But in America, we know that's not true. Look at our history.

Prompt

These two passages present different arguments regarding the issue of reducing greenhouse gas emissions. In your response, analyze both positions to determine which one is best supported. Use relevant and specific evidence from the passages to support your response.

Sample Response

These passages offer two significantly different views on how the United States should address its problem of greenhouse gas emissions. Both speakers concede that the United States is responsible for significant greenhouse gas emissions, and both speakers acknowledge the need for reducing these emissions. However, each speaker adopts a different attitude regarding implementation of such policies.

In this excerpt from President Bush's speech, he emphasizes the importance of an international, cooperative effort to deal with the problem. He does state that the United States generates one-fifth of the world's greenhouse gases. However, he quickly follows this information by stating that the United States is responsible for one-quarter of all economic activity, and then points out that four-fifths of the world's greenhouse gases are generated by other nations. By doing so, he attempts to explain the reason for high U.S. greenhouse emissions while also shifting the focus to other nations. Indeed, he goes on to point out how China and India are exempt from restricting greenhouse gas emissions, even though they are among the top greenhouse gas emitters.

Another key argument in Bush's speech emphasizes the economic perils of forcing drastic reductions in greenhouse gas emissions. Bush argues that to do so would devastate the U.S. economy, causing massive job layoffs and raising the cost of consumer goods. This argument also serves as the focal point in the excerpt from President Obama's speech. However, Obama refutes the claim that greenhouse gas restrictions will harm the economy. To support his position, Obama offers several historical examples where similar claims were made when businesses faced government-imposed restrictions. In each of those cases, the dire predictions of economic harm proved to be unfounded.

In essence, Bush's speech emphasizes fair play among all nations to ensure that the United States is not being held responsible for more than its share of the problem. Obama's speech emphasizes leadership by example, noting that the United States has successfully dealt with similar issues in the past. Of the two, I find Obama's position to be better supported through his use of historical examples. I also find his statement of leadership through action more compelling than Bush's call for fairness and cooperation.

Quiz

Now that you know what's involved in writing an effective essay, use what you've learned to answer the following questions.

1. What is the purpose of a prompt?
   a. to help the student start writing about the topic
   b. to state the main idea of the essay
   c. to provide support for the main idea
   d. to suggest a possible conclusion

2. Which of the following states the main idea of an essay?
   a. thesis statement
   b. transition
   c. topic sentence
   d. introduction

3. Which of the following sentences would be a good thesis statement?
   a. My favorite object is my grandfather's old leather bag.
   b. This is an essay about my favorite object.
   c. The bag is made of leather.
   d. My grandfather's leather bag

4. Why is it helpful to brainstorm when writing?
   a. It helps give you ideas of what to write about.
   b. It takes up time.
   c. It helps you write the thesis statement.
   d. It puts your ideas in order.

5. What is the purpose of creating an outline?
   a. to organize your ideas
   b. to take up time
   c. to practice your spelling
   d. to make revision unnecessary

6. Which of the following should always state the main idea of a paragraph?
   a. topic sentence
   b. transition
   c. thesis statement
   d. introduction

7. How many main ideas should a paragraph have?
   a. one
   b. two
   c. three
   d. no fewer than two

8. Which of the following is a purpose of supporting sentences?
   a. to provide examples
   b. to state the main idea
   c. to restate the thesis
   d. to give the reader a sense of closure

9. Which of the following should a good conclusion do?
   a. state a new idea
   b. end with a question
   c. use specific examples
   d. leave the reader with a sense of closure

10. What is the purpose of revising when writing?
   a. to move paragraphs
   b. to rewrite the essay
   c. to restate the thesis
   d. to correct minor errors

Answers

1. **a.** The prompt is meant to get you started thinking about the topic of your writing. As you write, your essay will address the prompt using details and support.

2. **a.** The thesis statement tells the main idea of the entire essay. Each paragraph contains a topic sentence that states the main idea of that paragraph.

3. **a.** The thesis statement should be a complete sentence that answers the question stated in the prompt.

4. **a.** Brainstorming helps you get all your ideas down on paper. After you brainstorm, you can choose which ideas to include and put these ideas in proper order.

5. **a.** An outline helps you organize your ideas and decide which will be the main ideas and which will be supporting details.

6. **a.** The topic sentence tells what the paragraph will be about. The rest of the sentences support the topic sentence.

7. **a.** Each paragraph should have one main idea. All of the sentences in the paragraph should explain or support that idea.

8. **a.** Supporting sentences help explain the main idea by providing examples and additional information.

9. **d.** The conclusion restates the main idea, wraps up the essay, and provides a sense of closure for the reader.

10. **d.** Revising is the step in which you correct errors in spelling, capitalization, and grammar. This is also the time to remove unrelated or unnecessary information, and clarify ideas as needed.

A Final Word

Whew! Throughout this book, you've reviewed a number of reading comprehension strategies that will help you do your best on the GED® Reasoning through Language Arts test. In this chapter, you've learned some tips that will help you do your best as you put the writing strategies into practice. You are on your way to earning an outstanding score on the test and bringing home the ultimate prize—your GED® test credential!

Certainly, remembering all this information and facing the GED® test can be intimidating, but you are taking all the right steps toward doing your best. Review these strategies until you are comfortable and confident in your abilities with each. Take the practice tests in this book and monitor your own learning. If there are skills you need to brush up on, go back to that section of the book and review the information. When you find skills that you have mastered, give yourself a pat on the back. You've earned it!

Keep the test-taking tips in this book in mind any time you take a test, not just the GED® test. Reading passages and answer choices carefully, paying attention to details, and selecting the one best answer choice are great ways to earn a top-notch score on any test. And don't sweat it when you come across a question that seems especially tough. It happens to everyone. Remember to carefully eliminate answer choices and look for grammatical clues before taking a guess. Furthermore, don't waste your time on questions you're just not sure of. Take a deep breath, mark your strongest guess, and move on. You can always come back at the end if time allows.

Remember, you're on the right track. Taking charge of your own learning and being prepared are great first steps toward a successful GED® test experience. Good luck!

In this chapter, you have reviewed strategies for writing an effective essay.

1. An **essay** has three main parts:
   - an introduction
   - a body
   - a conclusion

   You can think of these three parts as the beginning, middle, and end.

2. The **introduction** catches the reader's attention and introduces the main idea of the essay in the form of a thesis statement. The **body** develops the thesis statement in two or three paragraphs. The **conclusion** restates the thesis statement and brings the essay to a close.

3. The **writing** process has three main steps:
   - planning
   - writing
   - revising

4. **Planning** is an important step in the writing process. It helps you decide what you want to write about and organize your ideas effectively. Planning includes writing a thesis statement, brainstorming ideas, and then organizing them into an outline. Once you've completed these three steps, writing your essay should go more smoothly.

5. **Revising** gives you one last chance to make sure your essay is as good as it can be. If you have planned well, you should not have to make any major changes during the revision process. Some things to check for include capitalization, punctuation, repetition, and clarity.

8 ▶ RLA PRACTICE TEST 1

CHAPTER SUMMARY

Here is the first sample test based on the GED® Reasoning through Language Arts test. After working through the review in Chapters 3 through 7, take this test to see how much your score has improved from the diagnostic test in Chapter 2.

Like the diagnostic test, this practice test mirrors the real GED® Reasoning through Language Arts test. It consists of 50 items covering both reading and writing skills. For this practice test, time yourself. On test day, you will have 150 minutes (including a 10-minute break) to complete this part of the exam.

The answer sheet you should use for the multiple-choice questions is on the following page. Then comes the exam itself. After that is the answer key, in which each answer is explained to help you find out why the correct answers are right and why the incorrect answers are wrong.

Practice Test 1

1. ⓐ ⓑ ⓒ ⓓ
2. ⓐ ⓑ ⓒ ⓓ
3. ⓐ ⓑ ⓒ ⓓ
4. ⓐ ⓑ ⓒ ⓓ
5. ⓐ ⓑ ⓒ ⓓ
6. ⓐ ⓑ ⓒ ⓓ
7. ⓐ ⓑ ⓒ ⓓ
8. ⓐ ⓑ ⓒ ⓓ
9. ⓐ ⓑ ⓒ ⓓ
10. ⓐ ⓑ ⓒ ⓓ
11. ⓐ ⓑ ⓒ ⓓ
12. ⓐ ⓑ ⓒ ⓓ
13. ⓐ ⓑ ⓒ ⓓ
14. ⓐ ⓑ ⓒ ⓓ
15. ⓐ ⓑ ⓒ ⓓ
16. ⓐ ⓑ ⓒ ⓓ
17. ⓐ ⓑ ⓒ ⓓ

18. ⓐ ⓑ ⓒ ⓓ
19. ⓐ ⓑ ⓒ ⓓ
20. ⓐ ⓑ ⓒ ⓓ
21. ⓐ ⓑ ⓒ ⓓ
22. ⓐ ⓑ ⓒ ⓓ
23. ⓐ ⓑ ⓒ ⓓ
24. ⓐ ⓑ ⓒ ⓓ
25. ⓐ ⓑ ⓒ ⓓ
26. ⓐ ⓑ ⓒ ⓓ
27. ⓐ ⓑ ⓒ ⓓ
28. ⓐ ⓑ ⓒ ⓓ
29. ⓐ ⓑ ⓒ ⓓ
30. ⓐ ⓑ ⓒ ⓓ
31. ⓐ ⓑ ⓒ ⓓ
32. ⓐ ⓑ ⓒ ⓓ
33. ⓐ ⓑ ⓒ ⓓ
34. ⓐ ⓑ ⓒ ⓓ

35. ⓐ ⓑ ⓒ ⓓ
36. ⓐ ⓑ ⓒ ⓓ
37. ⓐ ⓑ ⓒ ⓓ
38. ⓐ ⓑ ⓒ ⓓ
39. ⓐ ⓑ ⓒ ⓓ
40. ⓐ ⓑ ⓒ ⓓ
41. ⓐ ⓑ ⓒ ⓓ
42. ⓐ ⓑ ⓒ ⓓ
43. ⓐ ⓑ ⓒ ⓓ
44. ⓐ ⓑ ⓒ ⓓ
45. ⓐ ⓑ ⓒ ⓓ
46. ⓐ ⓑ ⓒ ⓓ
47. ⓐ ⓑ ⓒ ⓓ
48. ⓐ ⓑ ⓒ ⓓ
49. ⓐ ⓑ ⓒ ⓓ
50. ⓐ ⓑ ⓒ ⓓ

Directions: Choose the *one best answer* to each question.

Questions 1 through 7 refer to the following excerpt from a novel.

What Does Daisy Want?

"It is a sad fact that I shall have to return to Geneva tomorrow."

"Well, Mr. Winterbourne," said Daisy, "I think you're horrid!"

(5) "Oh, don't say such awful things!" said Winterbourne, "Just at the last!"

"The last!" cried the young girl. "I call it the first. I have half a mind to leave you here and go straight back to the hotel alone." And

(10) for the next ten minutes, she did nothing but call him horrid.

Poor Winterbourne was confused. No young lady had ever been so upset by the announcement of his movements. His

(15) companion stopped paying any attention to Chillon Castle or the lake. She opened fire upon the mysterious charmer in Geneva whom she seemed to have decided he was hurrying back to see. How did Miss Daisy

(20) Miller know that there was a charmer in Geneva? Winterbourne was quite unable to discover.

And he was divided between being amazed at the quickness of her inference and

(25) being amused at the frankness of her chitchat. She seemed to him an extraordinary mixture of innocence and crudity.

"Does she never allow you more than

(30) three days at a time?" asked Daisy ironically. "Doesn't she give you a vacation in summer? There's no one so hard worked but they can get leave to go off somewhere at this season. I suppose, if you stay another day, she'll

(35) come after you in the boat. Do wait over till Friday, and I will go down to the landing to see her arrive!"

Winterbourne began to think he had been wrong about this young lady's

(40) temperament. If he had missed the personal accent, the personal accent was now making its appearance. It sounded very distinctly in her telling him she would stop "teasing" him if he would promise her to come to Rome in

(45) the winter.

"That's not a difficult promise to make," said Winterbourne. "My aunt has taken an apartment in Rome for the winter. She has already asked me to come and see

(50) her."

"I don't want you to come for your aunt," said Daisy. "I want you to come for me."

—Adapted from Henry James, *Daisy Miller*

1. Why is Daisy upset?
   a. She worries that Winterbourne is in love with her.
   b. She tends to be emotional about most things.
   c. She is worried about Winterbourne.
   d. She wants Winterbourne to pay more attention to her.

2. Which of the following best describes what Winterbourne thinks about Daisy?
   a. He dislikes the way she talks.
   b. He feels protective toward her.
   c. He is attracted to her passion.
   d. He is startled by her behavior.

3. Based on the excerpt, which description best characterizes the relationship between Winterbourne and Daisy?
   a. tense but caring
   b. lighthearted but practical
   c. fanciful and dreamlike
   d. indifferent but innocent

4. Based on the excerpt, what is Daisy most likely to do in the future?
   a. apologize to Winterbourne
   b. refuse to see Winterbourne again
   c. return to America at once
   d. make sure that Winterbourne visits her in Rome

5. How does the author depict Daisy?
   a. as a person with little emotion
   b. as someone who overreacts
   c. as someone with great humor
   d. as a person who is charitable

6. Which of the following best describes what Winterbourne means when he says, "Just at the last" (line 6)?
   a. He is leaving soon.
   b. He and Daisy are breaking up.
   c. He wants their relationship to end.
   d. He feels bitterness toward Daisy.

7. In which of the following ways are Daisy and Winterbourne alike?
   a. They are both irritable when upset.
   b. They are both worried about their future.
   c. They are both cutting their trips short.
   d. They are both curious about each other.

Questions 8 through 14 are based on the following passage.

Dear Editor:

(A)
(1) I am writing to tell you about a good Samaritan that should be given some recognition. (2) The other night I was driving to school in oak farms when my car broke down. (3) Luckily I was able to pull off the road without any problem since there was a large shoulder. (4) It was dark and I was worried that no one would see me, I put the emergency blinkers on. (5) My cell phone was dead and I couldn't call for help.

(B)
(6) Suddenly I saw a car slow down and park behind me. (7) Then a man got out of his car asked me if I was having car trouble, and offered to help me. (8) I told him that the car just died. (9) I said that my cell phone was dead too.

(C)
(10) He immediately picked up his cell phone and called a local gas station and then he waited with me until they came. (11) He drove me back to the gas station and stays until they were able to get the car going. (12) Gave me the bill, he picked it up and paid for everything. (13) I told him I wanted to pay him back, but, when I turned around, he had already left without even giving me his name. (14) I don't know who he was, but I was so grateful that I wanted to let everyone know that there are good Samaritans out there.

Sincerely,

Robin Malachosky

8. Sentence (1): I am writing to tell you about a good Samaritan <u>that should be</u> given some recognition.
   Which is the best way to write the underlined portion of the sentence?
   a. that would be
   b. whom should be
   c. which can be
   d. who should be

9. Sentence (2): The other night I was driving to school in oak farms when my car broke down.

Which correction should be made to sentence (2)?

a. change *driving* to *driven*

b. change *oak farms* to *Oak Farms*

c. change *broke* to *broken*

d. insert a comma after *school*

10. Sentence (4): It was dark and I was worried that no one would see me, I put the emergency blinkers on.

Which correction should be made to sentence (4)?

a. change *was* to *was being*

b. insert a comma after *worried*

c. remove the comma

d. insert *so* after the comma

11. Sentence (6): Suddenly I saw a <u>car slow down</u> and park behind me.

Which is the best way to write the underlined portion of the sentence? If the original is the best way, choose choice **a.**

a. car slow down

b. car slowed down

c. car is slowing down

d. car has slow down

12. Sentence (7): Then a man got out of his car asked me if I was having car trouble, and offered to help me.

Which correction should be made to sentence (7)?

a. remove the comma

b. change *asked* to *asks*

c. insert a comma after the first instance of *car*

d. change *was* to *were*

13. Sentences (8) and (9): I told him that the car just died. I said that my cell phone was dead too.

The most effective combination of sentences (8) and (9) would include which group of words?

a. and that my

b. so that my

c. which is why my

d. and that it was my

14. Sentence (11): He drove me back to the gas station <u>and stays until</u> they were able to get the car going.

Which is the best way to write the underlined portion of the sentence? If the original is the best way, choose choice **a.**

a. and stays until

b. and stays when

c. so he stays until

d. and stayed until

Questions 15 through 19 refer to the following excerpt from a short story.

Will She Land Her Jump?

"Ouch, that hurt," Yolanda said as she ended up falling on her side, yet again.

Her coach, Ellen, spoke. "What happened? You seemed to jump very well,
(5)   but then you lost it."

"I just don't seem to be able to get it. I jump high enough, but something happens and I can't land it," Yolanda answered, relacing her skates.
(10)   "I know it's not easy, but you can do it. You just have to visualize yourself flying through the air and landing. Think about it. See it in your head. You will get it, Yolanda. I promise you will," Ellen said.
(15)   Her coach had been with her since she was a little girl, always encouraging her to try

harder, jump higher, achieve more. She was like a family member to her. And like Ellen, Yolanda loved to skate and loved to compete.

(20) She wanted so much to get a chance at Nationals, but she had to land this jump, called an axel. It was required.

"That's it for today, Yolanda. See you tomorrow afternoon," Ellen said. It was

(25) already dark when Yolanda stood outside the arena waiting for her father to pick her up.

"How did it go?" he asked as she climbed
into the car.

"I still can't get the jump. Ellen told me

(30) to visualize it. She said I have to see myself doing it in my head before I will do it in reality."

"That sounds smart."

They arrived at home, and they all ate

(35) dinner—she, her father, and her mother. Yolanda turned in early. She fell asleep right away and started to dream. In the dream, she was an eagle that soared through the air and landed on a small rock in a large lake. It felt

(40) wonderful, sailing through the air and landing without any effort.

When she got up the next morning, she thought about her dream, and she started to imagine what it would be like to land the

(45) axel. It was in the back of her mind all day until she reached the arena.

Out on the ice, she felt a thrill of excitement as she picked up the speed needed to jump. Up, up, she went through

(50) the air. She flew and then turned just the right way, landing on one leg and then the other. It was magical.

"I did it! I did it!" she cried as Ellen came to give her a hug.

15. Based on the excerpt, what does Yolanda learn about mastering a jump?
   a. She learns that too much practice can be detrimental.
   b. She learns that she needs greater confidence.
   c. She learns that skating is an art form.
   d. She learns that she needs to practice more.

16. Which of the following best expresses the main idea of the excerpt?
   a. It takes a good deal of stamina to be an ice skater.
   b. Jumps, like life, are difficult to succeed at.
   c. Learning to skate is a lot like learning to swim.
   d. To do something difficult, it may be necessary to internalize it.

17. Which best describes the significance of the dream?
   a. It suggests that Yolanda enjoys flying.
   b. It suggests that Yolanda will become a great skater.
   c. It suggests that Yolanda will succeed with the jump.
   d. It shows that Yolanda is upset about her jump.

18. Based on the excerpt, what does Yolanda think of the dream?
   a. She sees herself soaring and landing like the eagle.
   b. She thinks that she can do anything she wants to do.
   c. She worries that she cannot do what the eagle did.
   d. She wonders at the meaning of the dream.

19. Which phrase best describes Yolanda?
   a. committed and receptive
   b. flighty but talented
   c. reluctant and nervous
   d. confident but practical

Questions 20 through 26 are based on the following passage.

The Oregon Trail

(A)

(1) The Oregon Trail abounds in history and lore. (2) As one of the major overland routes to the West Coast, it brings thousands of families to the Oregon Territory in search of free land. (3) The government was giving people large tracts of land free of charge, with married couples receiving 640 acres and single settlers got 320 acres.

(B)

(4) Often as many as 100 pioneers joined together to travel in wagons with canvas tops that were pulled by mules or oxen known as Prairie Schooners. (5) The trail began in independence, missouri, and usually started in April or May.

(C)

(6) The trip could take anywhere from four to six months. (7) The pioneers wanted to travel when the weather was the best and there was enough grass to support their teams. (8) They often followed the rivers and streams across the country this meant they would have fresh water along their way. (9) One of the hardest parts of the trip was getting across a river.

(D)

(10) The pioneers had to disassemble the wagons by taking them off its flat beds and floating them across the river like boats. (11) The pioneers coated the wagons with tar to make them waterproof.

(E)

(12) There were many dangers along the route including floods bad weather, illness, and Native American attacks. (13) Most people felt happy when they reached their destinations and could start their new lives.

20. Sentence (2): As one of the major overland routes to the West Coast, it brings thousands of families to the Oregon Territory in search of free land.

Which correction should be made to sentence (2)?
a. change *routes* to *route*
b. delete the comma
c. change *brings* to *brought*
d. change *West Coast* to *west coast*

21. Sentence (3): The government was giving people large tracts of land free of charge, with married couples receiving 640 acres and single settlers got 320 acres.

Which correction should be made to sentence (3)?
a. change *was giving* to *is giving*
b. insert a comma after *couples*
c. change *with* to *for*
d. change *got* to *getting*

22. Sentence (4): Often as many as 100 pioneers joined together to travel in wagons with canvas tops that were pulled by mules or oxen known as Prairie Schooners.

Which correction should be made to sentence 5?
a. change *joined* to *was joining*
b. insert a comma after *pulled*
c. move *known as Prairie Schooners* to after *canvas tops*
d. change *pulled* to *pulling*

23. Sentence (5): The trail began in <u>independence, missouri,</u> and usually started in April or May.

Which is the best way to write the underlined portion of this sentence?

a. Independence, Missouri
b. independence missouri,
c. Independence, Missouri,
d. Independence, missouri

24. Sentence (7): The pioneers wanted to travel when the weather was the best and there was enough grass to support their teams.

The most effective revision of sentence (7) would begin with which group of words?

a. As a result, the pioneers
b. In spite of that, the pioneers
c. Although the pioneers
d. Instead of the pioneers

25. Sentence (8): They often followed the rivers and streams across <u>the country this meant</u> they would have fresh water along their way.

Which is the best way to write the underlined portion of this sentence?

a. the country: instead of meaning
b. the country, this meant
c. the country, yet this meant
d. the country. This meant

26. Sentence (10): The pioneers had to disassemble the wagons by taking them off its flat beds and floating them across the river like boats.

Which correction should be made to sentence (10)?

a. insert a comma after *across*
b. change *take* to *taking*
c. change *disassemble* to *disassembled*
d. change *its* to *their*

Questions 27 through 32 refer to the following excerpt from an extended protection plan.

What Happens If It Breaks?

The Big Deal Protection Plan

2-Year Protection Plan—Extended Warranty

Plan #35671

(5) This is a contract that you have purchased to protect your XZ23 computer for a period of two years. Henceforth throughout the contract you will be referred to as "purchaser," and the Big Deal Protection Plan will be referred to as "provider." Your computer will be referred to as "product."

(10) Your purchase receipt contains the effective start date of this policy and must be shown before any work is undertaken on the machine.

Coverage

(15) The plan covers parts and labor costs to repair purchaser's product should such product fail to operate correctly due to:
■ defect in materials
■ dust or condensation
(20) ■ normal wear or tear
■ power surge

If provider determines that purchaser's product cannot be repaired, provider will replace it with a comparable product or
(25) reimburse purchaser for replacement of the product with a voucher card equal to the current retail value of the product as determined by provider.

In addition, purchaser can expect:
(30) ■ one battery repair or replacement when the original battery is defective as determined by provider
■ repair or replacement of chargers that were included in the original product

(35)
- one bulb replacement of purchaser's original bulb for desktop projectors
- repair of image burn-in for product monitors

Exclusions

(40) The plan does not cover the following:
- damage to purchaser's product caused by an accident, abuse, neglect, or intentional physical damage
- products that have been lost or stolen
(45)
- cosmetic damage to the product, such as scratches or dents
- damage to or loss of software
- any product with a serial number that has been altered

(50) **Service**

1. Visit bigdealprotection.com or call 1-800-BIG-DEAL to access information about service.

2. If purchaser has purchased a plan that
(55) provides for home service, purchaser will need to arrange this; otherwise, purchaser may need to bring the product to a repair shop.

3. Repairs and replacements will be done at
(60) provider's repair shop at provider's discretion.

4. If provider determines the product cannot be repaired, we will give purchaser a replacement within 30 days' time.

27. Based on the excerpt, which of the following will result in receiving a new computer?
- **a.** a lightning storm hitting the main drive
- **b.** water damage because of a hole in a roof
- **c.** virus destroying a word processing program
- **d.** dropping the computer when moving

28. Which of the following best restates the phrase "provider will replace it with a comparable product or reimburse purchaser for replacement of the product with a voucher card equal to the current retail value of the product as determined by provider" (lines 23 through 28)?
- **a.** The company will give the purchaser a similar computer or a credit for another computer that has the same value, which the company will figure out.
- **b.** The insurance company will ask the retailer to find a computer that has about the same value as the one that was sold to the purchaser.
- **c.** The company will give the purchaser another computer while they try to repair the broken computer, but it may not be the same make or model.
- **d.** The company will have its repair person assess the value of the computer and send the purchaser a check for that amount.

29. Which best describes the style in which this excerpt is written?
- **a.** detailed and technical
- **b.** casual
- **c.** lighthearted
- **d.** threatening

30. Which of the following best describes how the excerpt is organized?
- **a.** by listing the terms of the agreement in logical order
- **b.** by listing parts that are covered according to their cost
- **c.** by listing what is covered first and then what is not covered
- **d.** by listing the various problems that could occur and how to rectify them

31. What advantage does the purchaser have by taking out the extended warranty?
   a. The purchaser's coverage includes replacing a machine if it is stolen.
   b. The purchaser's coverage is longer and more thorough.
   c. The machine is covered for any problem that might arise.
   d. The purchaser's coverage ensures a new machine if the first one has a problem.

32. What might possibly happen if the purchaser does not have a receipt?
   a. An extra charge would be levied.
   b. It would complicate finding out about the coverage.
   c. It would lessen the extent of the contract.
   d. The purchaser would have to pay for repairs over a certain amount.

Questions 33 through 38 refer to the following excerpt from a novel.

Will She Marry Him?

It was Stewart Snyder whom she had always encouraged. He was so much manlier than the others; he was impressive, like his new ready-made suit with its padded shoulders.

(5) She sat with him upon a pile of presidential overshoes in the coat-closet under the stairs. As they drank two cups of coffee and nibbled at a chicken patty, the sounds of the orchestra seeped into the tiny room. Stewart

(10) whispered:

"I can't stand it, this breaking up after four years! College was the happiest time of our lives."

She believed it. "Oh, I know! To think

(15) that in just a few days we'll be parting, and we'll never see some of the bunch again!"

"Carol, you got to listen to me! You always duck when I try to talk seriously to you, but you got to listen to me. I'm going to

(20) be a big lawyer, maybe a judge, and I need you, and I'd protect you—"

His arm slid behind her shoulders. The insinuating music drained her independence. She said mournfully, "Would you take care of

(25) me?" She touched his hand. It was warm, solid.

"You bet I would! We'd have, we'd have bully times in Yankton, where I'm going to settle—"

(30) "But I want to do something with my life."

"What's better than making a comfy home and bringing up some cute kids and knowing nice, homey people?"

(35) "Of course. I know. I suppose that's so. Honestly, I do love children. But there's lots of women that can do housework, but I— well, if you have got a college education, you ought to use it for the world."

(40) "I know, but you can use it just as well in the home. And gee, Carol, just think of a bunch of us going out on a picnic some nice spring evening."

"Yes."

(45) "And sleigh-riding in winter, and going fishing—"

Blarrrrrrr! The orchestra had crashed into the "Soldiers' Chorus"; and she was protesting, "No! No! You're a dear, but I want

(50) to do things. I don't understand myself, but I want—everything in the world! Maybe I can't sing or write, but I know I can have an influence working in a library or school. Just suppose I encouraged some boy and he

(55) became a great artist! I will! I will do it! Stewart, dear, I can't settle down to nothing but dish-washing!"

After graduation she never saw Stewart Snyder again. She wrote to him once a

(60) week—for one month.

—Adapted from Sinclair Lewis, *Main Street* (1920)

33. Based on the excerpt, how would you describe Carol?

   a. fearless but needy

   b. emotional and changeable

   c. demure but determined

   d. fanciful and fun

34. Based on the information in the excerpt, Stewart would most likely participate in which of the following activities?

   a. go for a ride in the country on Sunday

   b. attend a political demonstration

   c. backpack through Europe

   d. attend a seminar on ancient art

35. How does the sound of the orchestra relate to the action of the scene?

   a. It helps the reader pay attention to the action.

   b. It emphasizes Carol's desire to do something with her life.

   c. It interrupts the exchange between Carol and Stewart.

   d. It mirrors Carol's strong feelings about settling down.

36. What is the most likely meaning of lines 59 and 60: "She wrote to him once a week—for one month"?

   a. It shows that their relationship was over.

   b. It shows the reader that Carol is irresponsible.

   c. It lets the reader know that Carol cared about Stewart.

   d. It emphasizes how little Carol and Stewart knew each other.

37. What effect does the fact that they are graduating have on the mood of the story?

   a. It suggests that the story is a metaphor for life.

   b. It shows how quickly life passes by.

   c. It gives the story more depth.

   d. It gives the story a sense of finality.

38. Which of the following is closest to the lesson the excerpt teaches?

   a. Ordinary life can be meaningful.

   b. Young people rarely know what they want.

   c. College makes individuals want to achieve great things.

   d. Individuals must find their own way.

Questions 39 through 43 refer to the following excerpt from a review.

Why Should We Clap Our Hands?

Clap your hands for *Clap Your Hands*, the new musical that opened Wednesday evening to raves from the audience. I was there for that magical evening of song and dance, and
(5)   unlike many musicals, this one even had a believable scenario.

     Marty (Ellen Dayton) and Jonnie (Irving Landers) were perfectly charming as the young couple who are thrown together
(10)   by circumstances and ultimately, after a long and difficult path, become stars of a new Broadway show. This show within a show plot might seem a bit hackneyed, but not in this instance. It worked perfectly because of
(15)   the natural talent the two have, not to mention the chemistry between them. It also allowed for some of the most creative show tunes and dance routines that I have heard or seen in recent memory.
(20)   Music and lyrics by Arthur Christianson shined, as did the choreography by Gianno Eliano. Perhaps the

only fault I could find was the chorus's too
avid background chatter, which proved to
(25)   distract from rather than enhance the many
scenes that they were in. But a bit more
direction by Matty Guerin would solve that
problem immediately.

The writing was crisp and the dialogue
(30)   filled with witty one-liners that would blow
away even the most critical malcontent. If
you decide to see this production, you will
also witness a show that features real
ensemble work that allows the energy of the
(35)   entire cast to shine, something most casts are
not capable of doing.

Even the children were terrific. Little
Lora (Wendy Caesar) is definitely a
showstopper when she belts out "Why Me?"
(40)   to the audience without any trace of
self-consciousness.

I guess you get the idea. For those who
didn't understand: This is the best musical
I've seen in about 20 years. I give it five
(45)   stars for its energy, creativity, and wonderful
talent, something that is rare in this day of
giant productions without much thought.
Make sure to see it.

39. What does the author suggest by lines 3 and 4:
"I was there for that magical evening of song
and dance"?
   a. that many other productions are tiresome
   b. that this production is about magic
   c. that some productions do not include music
   d. that the story line for the musical was hard
      to follow

40. Which of the following best describes the tone
of this excerpt?
   a. breezy but sobering
   b. sharp but enthusiastic
   c. humorous and direct
   d. clever but plodding

41. Which of the following best expresses the
author's opinion of the chorus?
   a. They did not help the production.
   b. They were bad actors.
   c. They had too many lines.
   d. They were unrehearsed.

42. Which of the following best describes the style
in which this review is written?
   a. methodical
   b. sophisticated
   c. technical
   d. flowery

43. Why does the author probably include the last
paragraph?
   a. to make sure the reader gets the main point
      of the review
   b. to indicate that his writing is difficult to
      understand
   c. to show that he is knowledgeable about
      musicals
   d. to emphasize why musicals are agreeable

*Questions 44 through 50 are based on the following
passage.*

How to Dress for an Interview

(A)

(1) The clothes you choose for an interview
definitely make a difference, they express
who you are and what you think of yourself.
(2) The first impression you make on an
interviewer means a great deal and if you
come in an outfit that doesn't look neat and
clean, it could mean the interview will be cut
very short.

(B)

(3) Whether to ware a suit or not to an
interview depends on the circumstances.

(4) If you are looking for a job as a teacher and you are a man, you probably should put on a suit, while, if you are woman, you should also dress in a professional manner. (5) That means jackets skirts, and stockings for the women and ties for the men.

(C)

(6) However, if you are applying to be a car technician or to work for a fire department, you didn't have to be quite so dressy. (7) You can dress in something a bit more casual, but still attractive. (8) Make sure to bring your résumé with you. (9) Khaki trousers and a dress shirt for the guys would be fine and, for the women, a nice skirt and top will do. (10) As for jeans, unless you are planning to work for someone who makes jeans, leave it at home.

(D)

(11) If you have tattoos, it might want be best to cover them with clothing. (12) It depends, of course, on who is interviewing you. (13) The same goes for body piercings. (14) You might want to remove them for the interview, and if you get the job, remove them while you are at work. (15) In general, interviewers like potential employees to dress like them or at least like their other employees. (16) The people who do best on interviews dress conservatively. (17) Leave your wild side at home.

44. Sentence (1): The clothes you choose for an interview definitely make a difference, they express who you are and what you think of yourself.

  Which correction should be made to sentence (1)?

  a. change *makes* to *made*
  b. insert a comma after *choose*
  c. remove the comma
  d. change the comma to a semicolon

45. Sentence (3): Whether to ware a suit or not to an interview depends on the circumstances.

  Which correction should be made to sentence (3)?

  a. change *Whether* to *Weather*
  b. change *ware* to *wear*
  c. change *depends* to *depend*
  d. change *circumstances* to *circumstantial*

46. Sentence (5): That means <u>jackets skirts, and stockings</u> for the women and ties for the men.

  Which is the best way to write the underlined portion of this sentence?

  a. jackets: skirts; and stockings
  b. jackets, skirts, and stockings
  c. jackets skirts and stockings
  d. jackets: skirts and stockings

47. Sentence (6): However, if you are applying to be a car technician or to work for a fire department, you didn't have to be quite so dressy.

  Which correction should be made to sentence (6)?

  a. change *didn't* to *don't*
  b. change to *work* to *working*
  c. change *dressy* to *dressier*
  d. insert a comma after *car*

48. Sentence (10): As for jeans, unless you are planning to work for someone who makes jeans, <u>leave it</u> at home.

  Which is the best way to write the underlined portion of this sentence?

  a. leaving it
  b. leaves it
  c. leave them
  d. leaves them

49. Which revision should be made to paragraph (C)?

  a. remove sentence (6)

  b. move sentence (7) to the end of the paragraph

  c. remove sentence (8)

  d. start a new paragraph after sentence (6)

50. Sentence (11): If you have tattoos, <u>it might want be</u> best to cover them with clothing.

  Which is the best way to write the underlined portion of this sentence?

  a. they could be

  b. it might be

  c. it might should be

  d. they might be

Read the following passage. Then, read the prompt and write an essay taking a stance. Use information from the passage to support your essay.

NASA Funding

Government funding for the National Aeronautics and Space Administration, better known as NASA, has long been a source of controversy. When adjusted for inflation, funding for NASA has been relatively flat since the 1990s; as a percentage of the total federal budget, however, spending for NASA has been on a steady decline, accounting for less than one-half of one percent of the federal budget in 2012. The issue of whether or not the federal government should fund a space program at all is a divisive one. Supporters of NASA argue that the benefits of a space program far outweigh the significant financial burdens. Opponents argue that the money could be better spent on dealing with problems closer to home.

Those that argue in favor of increasing funding for NASA point out that the program's many benefits far outweigh its relatively tiny budget. First and foremost, NASA missions have greatly expanded humanity's understanding of the Universe. When most people think of NASA, they think of manned missions to the Moon and aboard the Space Shuttles, which in themselves have yielded amazing information and discoveries. However, satellites, observers, and rovers have also been sent across the solar system to provide detailed images and data about celestial bodies both near and far away. Voyager 2, for example, has traveled beyond the orbit of Pluto, and continues to transmit data back to Earth as it continues toward the outer reaches of our solar system. The Hubble Space Telescope, while remaining closer to Earth, has provided scientists with the most detailed images of the Universe ever recorded, resulting in countless new discoveries.

On a more practical level, many of the technologies developed for NASA have led to consumer products that directly benefit economic growth and quality of life for all Americans. Things like memory foam, invisible braces, and scratch-resistant eyeglass lenses were all developed thanks to NASA innovations. Products developed by and for NASA, such as infrared thermometers, cordless drills, and water filters, later made their way to consumers and spurred the growth of private industry.

Arguments against funding for NASA tend to focus on its impracticality. With so many pressing social issues in the United States, such as unemployment and skyrocketing health care costs, some feel the money spent on NASA would be better spent to address those problems instead. While NASA's funding remains a tiny part of the overall federal budget, it still amounts to billions of dollars. Most of its standout missions take several years to plan, and some of these high-profile projects have resulted in failure or disaster. In 1986, the Space Shuttle Challenger exploded shortly after takeoff, killing all seven crew members; in 2003, another shuttle, the Columbia, disintegrated on re-entry, also resulting in the deaths of all seven crew members. The Hubble Space Telescope was famously flawed, with an incorrectly ground mirror, when it was put into space in 1990. This required an additional space mission three years later to repair it.

Another argument used against NASA is that there is still plenty of scientific research left to be done on Earth. The deep ocean, for example, has proven to be a more elusive field of study than outer space. Even beyond physical exploration, scientific fields such as genetics and cancer research could use the funding in ways that might provide a more direct benefit to humankind.

Prompt

This passage presents different arguments regarding the issue of NASA funding. In your response, analyze both positions to determine which one is best supported. Use relevant and specific evidence from the passages to support your response.

Answers

1. d. While some of the choices may seem attractive, the real reason that Daisy is upset is that she wants Winterbourne to pay more attention to her. She turns on him when she thinks he is paying another woman more attention than she is receiving.

2. d. Winterbourne is definitely startled by Daisy's behavior because she changed her way of dealing with him so abruptly.

3. a. This is the best description of what is going on between Daisy and Winterbourne in the excerpt. They seem to be caring toward each other, but the scene is definitely tense.

4. d. This is clearly a priority for Daisy. The other choices are not supported by the passage. She certainly is not going to apologize, and there is no reason to believe she will leave for America or refuse to see Winterbourne again.

5. b. This is the best answer. Daisy may be a tiny bit jealous, but she definitely overreacts. She is dramatic in what she does and says.

6. a. This is the meaning of "Just at the last." The excerpt makes it clear that Winterbourne is leaving soon, but there is no mention or suggestion that he is breaking up with her, or that he feels bitterness toward her.

7. d. Daisy and Winterbourne are both curious about the other. This answer is supported by the excerpt in the way they want to find out about each other.

8. d. Choice **d** is correct because the pronoun *who* refers to a person and not a thing or animal. Both *that* and *which* do not refer to a person. Choice **b** has the correct verb form but an incorrect pronoun, while choices **a** and **c** have an incorrect verb form.

9. b. Choice **b** is correct. Proper names should be capitalized. Choices **a** and **c** have incorrect verb forms, and choice **d** would insert an unnecessary comma.

10. d. Choice **d** is correct because the coordinating conjunction *so* makes the comma splice a compound sentence. Choice **a** changes a correct verb form into an incorrect one. Choice **b** inserts an unnecessary comma. Choice **c** would create a run-on sentence.

11. a. Choice **a** is correct. This is the correct form of the verb. It corresponds to the verb *park*. All the other choices have incorrect verb forms and do not correspond to *park*.

12. c. Choice **c** is correct. This is a list of actions, and each one needs to be separated by a comma in the same way other lists are. Choice **a** removes a needed comma. Choices **b** and **d** have incorrect verb tenses.

13. a. Choice **a** is correct. Choices **b** and **c** change the meaning of the sentences. Choice **d** creates a confusing sentence.

14. d. Choice **d** is correct. This has the correct tense (past), which matches the verb *drove*. Choice **a** has an incorrect present tense, as does choice **c**. Choice **b** has an incorrect tense, and the word *when* jumbles the meaning of the sentence.

15. b. This is what Yolanda learns. There is no suggestion that too much practice is detrimental, or bad, for her. She probably already knows that skating is an art form, and she certainly practices enough.

16. d. Yolanda had to internalize doing the jump before she could do it. That is why she had her dream. Although choices **a** and **c** are probably true, they are not the main idea of the passage.

17. c. This answer reflects the meaning of the dream—that Yolanda could feel herself soaring through the air. It helps her master the jump.

18. a. This is how she sees herself in the dream and even after she wakes up. She has a good feeling about making the jump.

19. a. Based on the excerpt, the reader can determine that Yolanda is committed and receptive. This is the best description of her.

20. c. Choice **c** is correct. It changes a present tense verb to the correct past tense. Choice **a** is an incorrect change to a singular form of the noun. Choice **b** would create a run-on sentence, and choice **d** would incorrectly lowercase a specific region.

21. d. Choice **d** is correct. This change creates parallel construction with the verb *receiving*. Choice **a** is incorrect because the verb is in the present tense. Choice **b** inserts an unnecessary comma. Choice **c** inserts an incorrect preposition.

22. c. Choice **c** is correct. This phrase is a modifier for *wagons with canvas tops*, not mules or oxen, so it needs to be immediately after it. Choice **a** creates an incorrect verb choice and is singular rather than plural. Choice **b** inserts an unnecessary comma. Choice **d** is also an incorrect verb.

23. c. Choice **c** is correct. Names of cities and states should be capitalized and separated by a comma. Choice **a** deletes both commas incorrectly. Choice **b** is wrong because it does not capitalize either the city or the state and incorrectly deletes the comma between the city and state. Choice **d** doesn't capitalize both proper names.

24. a. Choice **a** is correct. This beginning links sentence (7) to sentence (6). None of the others show the correct relationship between the two sentences.

25. d. Choice **d** is correct. This is a run-on sentence that needs to be divided into two distinct sentences. Choice **b** is a comma splice. Choices **a** and **c** join the two sentences with inappropriate conjunctions.

26. d. Choice **d** is correct. The possessive pronoun *its* does not agree with the noun *wagons* and should be changed to *their*. Choice **a** is incorrect because it inserts an unnecessary comma. Choices **b** and **c** have verbs in the wrong form.

27. a. If you read the plan carefully, you will see that a power surge, such as a lightning strike, could result in receiving a new computer. The other options are not listed as being covered. None of the other choices are caused by normal wear or tear, defective materials, or dust or condensation, which are listed as covered as well.

28. a. This is a restatement of the information in the protection plan. It is the only choice that states that the company will replace the computer if necessary and explains exactly what will happen if the computer cannot be fixed.

29. a. The way in which the protection plan is written is extremely *detailed and technical* because it lists so much information about what may happen to the computer and what is covered. The style certainly isn't *lighthearted*, *threatening*, or *casual*.

30. c. This is the way the protection plan is organized—listing what is covered and then what is not covered. It is not organized in the manner suggested by the other choices.

31. b. The reader can figure out that the coverage for the extended plan is longer and more thorough than the normal plan that might come with the computer. The other choices might be possible, but they are not correct.

32. b. It would stand to reason that the warranty would still be valid, but it would be more complicated to access it. The other choices are not supported by the plan.

33. c. This choice best describes Carol. She keeps things to herself for the most part, but she is clearly determined. She doesn't seem at all needy or changeable.

34. a. It seems clear from Stewart's idea of his life that this would be most logical choice for him. Backpacking or attending a political demonstration do not seem as likely for him, and neither does going to a seminar on ancient art.

35. d. The music acts as a reflection of the tension that Carol feels in the excerpt. It reflects her feelings about settling down with Stewart and her outburst of "No! No!"

36. a. The fact that she stopped writing after "one month" demonstrates that the relationship, like the letter writing, was over. It is obvious that she did not want to settle down with Stewart.

37. d. There is a sense of finality because their graduation marks the end of their school years together. This is the best answer. It is not a metaphor for life, nor does it suggest how short life is.

38. d. This is the best answer. Carol had to go her own way. College may make some people want to achieve great things (choice **c**), but not everyone.

39. a. The reviewer loved this musical, which is why he thought it was "magical" in the "fantastic and wonderful" sense of the word. Choice **b** uses the word *magic*, but not the way the reviewer intended. Since this play was so wonderful, it can be assumed that not all plays the reviewer sees are wonderful and that many are boring or tiresome.

40. b. This is the tone of the review. Some of the comments are *sharp*, but most of them are *enthusiastic*. The review certainly is not *sobering* or *plodding*. It might have been somewhat *humorous*, but it is not *direct*.

41. a. This is what the author means when he talks about the chorus.

42. b. The review is written in a sophisticated style; the language is not simple, and the author is very knowledgeable about theater.

43. a. This is the intent of the last paragraph: to emphasize what the author's opinion is. He is re-emphasizing his main point, which was that the play should be seen by anyone remotely interested in theater.

44. d. Choice **d** is correct because the semicolon transforms the comma splice into two independent sentences. Choice **a** changes a correct verb form into an incorrect one. Choice **b** inserts an unnecessary comma. Choice **c** would create a run-on sentence.

45. b. Choice **b** is correct. The spelling of the homonym that is used has the wrong meaning for the context of the sentence. Choice **a** is incorrect because it substitutes an incorrect homonym in place of the correct one. Choice **c** is incorrect because the verb does not agree with the subject of the sentence. Choice **d** transforms the correct word to an incorrect one.

46. b. Choice **b** is correct. Items in a list need to have commas after them. Choice **a** inserts both a colon and a semicolon incorrectly. Choice **c** has no commas. Choice **d** inserts a colon incorrectly.

47. a. Choice **a** is correct. This changes the verb tense to the present. Choice **b** incorrectly changes the verb tense. Choice **c** is an incorrect adjective form, and choice **d** would insert an unnecessary comma.

48. c. Choice **c** is correct. The pronoun refers to "jeans," which is plural and should also be plural. Choice **a** uses a singular pronoun and an incorrect verb. Choice **b** uses a singular pronoun and incorrectly changes the verb to a singular form. Choice **d** has the correct pronoun but an incorrect verb.

49. c. Choice **c** is correct. This sentence has nothing to do with the topic of how to dress for an interview. Choice **a** is wrong because sentence (6) is a needed topic sentence. Choice **b** creates confusion, as does choice **d**.

50. b. Choice **b** is correct. The terms *could* and *should* are all unneeded, which eliminates choices **a** and **c**. Choice **d** has an incorrect pronoun.

Extended Response

For this prompt, an extended response should focus on the pros and cons of NASA funding. The passage is already conveniently arranged to allow for an easy summation of the important points on each side of the issue. However, a successful extended response should not be limited to simply restating the points presented. In addition, it should analyze the arguments presented by each side. In this case, both sides present arguments that are based on practicality and common sense. Both sides use very specific examples to support their points—such as Voyager 2, the Hubble Space Telescope, and the Challenger disaster—and these should be called out in the extended response. It should also be noted that neither side offers a direct refutation of the facts presented by the other side. In essence, the pro argument asserts that money spent on NASA yields worthwhile results, while the con side argues that there are probably better ways to spend the same money. This shows a weakness in the con side of the argument, since the examples offered, such as undersea exploration and cancer research, are not guaranteed to yield worthwhile results either. However, a successful extended response could be written in support of either viewpoint.

9 ▶ RLA PRACTICE TEST 2

CHAPTER SUMMARY

Here is the second sample test based on the GED® Reasoning through Language Arts test. After working through the review in Chapters 3 through 7, take this test to see how much your score has improved from the diagnostic test in Chapter 2.

L ike the diagnostic test, this practice test is of the same type as the GED® Reasoning through Language Arts test. It consists of 50 items covering both reading and writing skills. For this practice test, time yourself. On test day, you will have 150 minutes (including a 10-minute break) to complete this part of the exam.

The answer sheet you should use for the multiple-choice questions is on the following page. Then comes the exam itself. After that is the answer key, in which each answer is explained to help you find out why the correct answers are right and why the incorrect answers are wrong.

Practice Test 2

1. (a) (b) (c) (d)
2. (a) (b) (c) (d)
3. (a) (b) (c) (d)
4. (a) (b) (c) (d)
5. (a) (b) (c) (d)
6. (a) (b) (c) (d)
7. (a) (b) (c) (d)
8. (a) (b) (c) (d)
9. (a) (b) (c) (d)
10. (a) (b) (c) (d)
11. (a) (b) (c) (d)
12. (a) (b) (c) (d)
13. (a) (b) (c) (d)
14. (a) (b) (c) (d)
15. (a) (b) (c) (d)
16. (a) (b) (c) (d)
17. (a) (b) (c) (d)

18. (a) (b) (c) (d)
19. (a) (b) (c) (d)
20. (a) (b) (c) (d)
21. (a) (b) (c) (d)
22. (a) (b) (c) (d)
23. (a) (b) (c) (d)
24. (a) (b) (c) (d)
25. (a) (b) (c) (d)
26. (a) (b) (c) (d)
27. (a) (b) (c) (d)
28. (a) (b) (c) (d)
29. (a) (b) (c) (d)
30. (a) (b) (c) (d)
31. (a) (b) (c) (d)
32. (a) (b) (c) (d)
33. (a) (b) (c) (d)
34. (a) (b) (c) (d)

35. (a) (b) (c) (d)
36. (a) (b) (c) (d)
37. (a) (b) (c) (d)
38. (a) (b) (c) (d)
39. (a) (b) (c) (d)
40. (a) (b) (c) (d)
41. (a) (b) (c) (d)
42. (a) (b) (c) (d)
43. (a) (b) (c) (d)
44. (a) (b) (c) (d)
45. (a) (b) (c) (d)
46. (a) (b) (c) (d)
47. (a) (b) (c) (d)
48. (a) (b) (c) (d)
49. (a) (b) (c) (d)
50. (a) (b) (c) (d)

Directions: Choose the *one best answer* to each question.

Questions 1 through 7 refer to the following excerpt from a novel.

Will She Let Him Help Her?

"My goodness—you can't go on living here!" Rosedale exclaimed.

(5) Lily smiled. "I am not sure that I can, either; but I have gone over my expenses very carefully, and I rather think I shall be able to manage it."

"Be able to manage it? That's not what I mean—it's no place for you!"

"It's what I mean. I have been out of (10) work for the last week."

"Out of work—out of work! What a way for you to talk! The idea of your having to work—it's preposterous." He brought out his sentences in short violent jerks, as though (15) they were forced up from a deep inner crater of indignation. "It's a farce—a crazy farce," he repeated, his eyes fixed on the long vista of the room reflected in the glass between the windows.

(20) Lily continued to meet his arguments with a smile. "I don't know why I should regard myself as an exception—" she began.

"Because you *are*; that's why. And your being in a place like this is an outrage. I can't (25) talk of it calmly."

She had in truth never seen him so shaken
out of his usual glibness. There was something almost moving to her in his inarticulate struggle with his emotions.

(30) He rose with a start, which left the rocking chair quivering on its beam ends, and placed himself squarely before her.

"Look here, Miss Lily, I'm going to Europe next week: going over to Paris and (35) London for a couple of months—and I can't leave you like this. I can't do it. I know it's none of my business—you've let me understand that often enough—but things are worse with you now than they have been (40) before, and you must see that you've got to accept help from somebody. You spoke to me the other day about some debt to Trenor. I know what you mean—and I respect you for feeling as you do about it."

(45) A blush of surprise rose to Lily's pale face, but before she could interrupt him, he had continued eagerly: "Well, I'll lend you the money to pay Trenor; and I won't—I—see here, don't take me up till I've finished. (50) What I mean is, it'll be a plain business arrangement, such as one man would make with another. Now, what have you got to say against that?"

—Adapted from Edith Wharton, *The House of Mirth*

1. Why is Rosedale upset?
   a. Lily is out of work and cannot pay her rent.
   b. Lily is living in a place he thinks is beneath her.
   c. Lily will not accept him as a suitor.
   d. Lily will not do what he wants her to do.

2. How does Lily react to what Rosedale says?
   a. She is impressed but also embarrassed.
   b. She thinks he is much too forward.
   c. She is worried the arrangement will not work out.
   d. She believes that he is dangerous.

3. Based on the excerpt, what can the reader infer about Lily?
  a. She is afraid of her future.
  b. She has no educational background.
  c. She is needy and requires others' kindnesses.
  d. She is very proud and independent.

4. Which of the following best explains why Rosedale says that Lily's being out of work is "a farce"?
  a. He believes she should not have to work.
  b. He thinks that no women should work.
  c. He believes she made the job up.
  d. He wants to marry her.

5. Based on the excerpt, which best describes Rosedale?
  a. rude and self-involved
  b. blunt and determined
  c. cautious and mannered
  d. sympathetic but shy

6. What is the mood of the excerpt?
  a. carefree
  b. romantic
  c. depressed
  d. intense

7. What is implied about the relationship between Lily and Rosedale in the past?
  a. She was unaware that he cared about her.
  b. She was not interested in him as a suitor.
  c. She hardly knew him at all until recently.
  d. She liked him but thought he did not care for her.

Questions 8 through 13 are based on the following passage.

Dear Mr. Anderson:

(A)

(1) I am writing to you to apply for the position of computer technician who was advertised in the local newspaper. (2) Although I never studied computer repair formally, I have a lot of experience to repair computers for people. (3) You might say I am self-taught. (4) Have been involved with tinkering with computers since I was a kid.

(B)

(5) I hope one day to be a computer programmer. (6) I will be entering fairfield technical school in the fall to study programming, so a summer job would be just right for me. (7) Perhaps I could work part-time after school starts. (8) I am familiar with both PC and Apple computers.

(C)

(9) I would like to meat with you and discuss the job farther. (10) I has three excellent references from people, who are professionals. (11) I am including my résumé, which has my phone number email address and mailing address. (12) I look forward to hearing from you.

Sincerely yours,

Marco Doria

8. Sentence (1): I am writing to you to apply for the position of computer technician who was advertised in the local newspaper.

What correction should be made to sentence (1)?

a. change *writing* to *written*
b. insert a comma after *technician*
c. change *who* to *that*
d. change *newspaper* to *Newspaper*

9. Sentence (4): Have been involved with tinkering with computers since I was a kid.

Which correction should be made to sentence (4)?

a. insert *I* and change *Have* to *have*
b. change *involved* to *involving*
c. insert *He* and change *Have* to *have*
d. change *was* to *were*

10. Sentence (6): I will be entering <u>fairfield technical school</u> in the fall to study programming, so a summer job would be just right for me.

Which is the best way to write the underlined portion of the sentence?

a. fairfield Technical School
b. Fairfield technical school
c. Fairfield Technical, school
d. Fairfield Technical School

11. Sentence (9): I would like to meat with you and discuss the job farther.

Which correction should be made to sentence (9)?

a. change *like* to *liking* and *meat* to *meet*
b. change *meat* to *meet* and *farther* to *further*
c. change *like* to *liking* and *discuss* to *discussing*
d. change *discuss* to *discussing* and *meat* to *meet*

12. Sentence (10): I has three excellent references from people, who are professionals.

Which correction should be made to sentence (10)?

a. change *has* to *have* and delete comma
b. change *references* to *references'* and *has* to *have*
c. insert a comma after *references*
d. change *has* to *have* and *who* to *that*

13. Sentence (11): I am including my résumé, which has my <u>phone number email address and</u> mailing address.

Which is the best way to write the underlined portion of the sentence?

a. phone number email address and
b. phone number email address, and
c. phone number, email address, and
d. phone number; email address, and

Questions 14 through 18 refer to the following excerpt from a novel.

Why Does She Want to Go?

The voice seemed to come from the dark shadows at the end of the garden. The singer sang slowly, his voice lingering caressingly on the words. The last verse died away softly

(5) and clearly, almost imperceptibly fading into silence.

For a moment, there was utter stillness, then Diana lay back with a little sigh. "The Kashmiri Song. It makes me think of India. I

(10) heard a man sing it in Kashmir last year, but not like that. What a wonderful voice!"

Arbuth looked at her curiously, surprised at the sudden ring of interest in her tone and the animation of her face.

(15)   "You say you have no emotion in your nature, and yet that unknown man's singing has stirred you deeply. How do you reconcile the two?" he asked, almost angrily.

(20)   "Is an appreciation of the beautiful emotion?" she challenged, with uplifted eyes. "Surely not. Music, art, nature, everything beautiful appeals to me. But there is nothing emotional in that. It is only that I prefer beautiful things to ugly ones. For that reason,

(25)   even pretty clothes appeal to me," she added, laughing.

   "You are the best-dressed woman in Biskra," he noted. "But is not that a concession to the womanly feelings that you

(30)   despise?"

   "Not at all. To take an interest in one's clothes is not an exclusively feminine vice. I like pretty dresses. I admit to spending some time in thinking of color schemes to go with

(35)   my horrible hair, but I assure you that my dressmaker has an easier life than my brother's tailor."

   She sat silent, hoping that the singer might not have gone, but there was no sound

(40)   except a cicada chirping near her. She swung round in her chair, looking in the direction from which it came. "Listen to him. Jolly little chap! They are the first things I listen for when I get to Port Said. They mean the

(45)   East to me."

   "Maddening little beasts!" said Arbuth irritably.

   "They are going to be very friendly little beasts to me during the next four

(50)   weeks. . . . You don't know what this trip means to me. I like wild places. The happiest times of my life have been spent camping in America and India, and I have always wanted the desert more than either of them. It is

(55)   going to be a month of pure joy. I am going to be enormously happy."

—Adapted from Edith Hull, *The Sheik* (1921)

14. In what way is Diana's response to the song similar to her response to the sound of the cicada?
a. She is unfamiliar with both of them.
b. She thinks their sounds are similar.
c. They remind her of faraway places.
d. They bring up frightening emotions.

15. What is the mood of the passage?
a. reflective
b. troubled
c. quarrelsome
d. sorrowful

16. Based on the information in the passage, which of the following pairs of words best describes Diana?
a. independent and passionate
b. reckless and thoughtless
c. taunting and hurtful
d. considerate and helpful

17. Why does Arbuth react angrily to what Diana says about the music?
a. He thinks she is a difficult woman.
b. He believes she is very feminine.
c. He wants her to give up her plans.
d. He believes that she is lying about herself.

18. Based on what is known about Diana, what is the most likely reason for her traveling to the desert?
   a. for business
   b. on a whim
   c. to meet her husband
   d. to fulfill a promise

Questions 19 through 25 are based on the following passage.

Manatees

(A)

(1) Manatees are really interesting animals. (2) They are also called sea cows. (3) Their size is remarkable with some manatees measuring as long as 12 feet and weigh as much as 1,200 pounds. (4) They mostly eats sea grass and they are quite friendly.

(B)

(5) Early sailors thought that manatees was mermaids. (6) The sailors usually viewed the manatees underwater, they can't come to the surface. (7) They probably imagine that these creatures were the ones that they heard about from other sailors. (8) Christopher Columbus new that sailors thought they were mermaids. (9) He even wrote in his journal about them.

(C)

(10) Long ago, manatees were hunted by the Taino people in the Caribbean for its skins. (11) Today they are endangered. (12) Boats hit them or they are hurt by the propellers. (13) They are protected by laws making it illegal to hurt them.

19. Sentences (1) and (2): Manatees are really interesting animals. They are also called sea cows.

   The most effective way of combining sentences (1) and (2) would include which group of words?
   a. however, they are called
   b. such as sea cows
   c. as a result, they are called
   d. that are also called

20. Sentence (3): Their size is remarkable with some manatees measuring as long as 12 feet and weigh as much as 1,200 pounds.

   Which correction should be made to sentence (3)?
   a. change *their* to *there*
   b. change *is* to *are*
   c. change *measuring* to *measures*
   d. change *weigh* to *weighing*

21. Sentence (4): <u>They mostly eats</u> sea grass and they are quite friendly.

   Which is the best way to write the underlined portion of the sentence?
   a. They mostly were eating
   b. They most eat
   c. They sometimes eat
   d. They mostly eat

22. Sentence (6): The sailors usually viewed the manatees underwater, they can't come to the surface.

   Which correction should be made to sentence (6)?
   a. change *viewed* to *view*
   b. insert a comma after *manatees*
   c. remove the comma
   d. replace the comma with *since*

23. Sentence (7): They <u>probably imagine</u> that these creatures were the ones that they heard about from other sailors.

Which is the best way to write the underlined portion of this sentence?
a. probably will imagine
b. couldn't imagine
c. probably imagined
d. probably was imagining

24. Sentence (8): Christopher Columbus new that sailors thought they were mermaids.

Which correction should be made to sentence (8)?
a. change *new* to *knew*
b. change *sailors* to *sailors'*
c. change *thought* to *think*
d. change *were* to *are*

25. Sentence (10): Long ago, manatees were hunted by the Taino people in the Caribbean for its skins.

Which correction should be made to sentence 10?
a. insert a comma after *hunted*
b. change *were hunted* to *was hunted*
c. change *Taino* to *taino*
d. change *its* to *their*

Questions 26 through 31 refer to the following excerpt from a company handbook.

How Will This Program Help You?

Here at Coralis, we consider our employees like a family, and to that point we are instituting a new program that will help employees improve their health by staying (5) fit. We are in the process of creating a 3,000 square-foot, on-site gym in Building G that will offer classes in yoga and mat Pilates as well as workout equipment and personal trainers. The facility can be utilized before, (10) after, and even during employee work hours.

After exhaustive research, our Health and Fitness Committee agreed that a company gym would offer the best option for our employees who may find it hard to fit (15) in a workout schedule when they have such a busy load of work to accomplish each day. This gym will replace our arrangement with the Fitness Today facility, which employees were encouraged to use in the past. Use of (20) the gym, as well as classes, is included as part of each employee's salary. To start, classes will be given at 8 A.M., 12 noon, and 5 P.M. General workout is available throughout the day. Personal trainers will be paid by both (25) the company and individuals, with employees paying half of the cost.

In addition to the facility, there will be an incentive program for taking part in gym activities. Each workout session will result in (30) the employee receiving a token. Accumulated tokens can be redeemed at the company cafeteria. Of course, the kind of foods that they can be redeemed for will be "heart healthy" choices such as salads, low-fat (35) meals, fruits, and vegetables. Other items may be purchased with cash.

We feel that the institution of this stellar program will go far to improve the fitness of each employee. This will doubtless (40) have a positive impact on employee production. We will also be hosting goal programs, such as weight loss and strength training initiatives. We look forward to your input about the new gym and its associated (45) activities. We at Coralis like to be first in proactive ways to keep our employees not only fit, but also happy.

26. Based on the excerpt, what can be inferred about the management of Coralis?
   a. They believe the program will improve the amount of work each employee produces.
   b. They believe the program will benefit the company by making employees less competitive.
   c. They believe the exercise program will make employees work longer hours.
   d. They believe the program will make employees more confident.

27. Which of the following would the new exercise program most likely help?
   a. a person who has trouble staying on a diet
   b. a person who has difficulty concentrating
   c. a person going through a personal crisis
   d. a person who enjoys competitive sports

28. Who is most likely to use a personal trainer?
   a. a temporary worker
   b. a salesperson who travels a lot
   c. an executive who works odd hours
   d. a person who likes classroom settings

29. Based on the excerpt, what does the token incentive system most likely have as a goal?
   a. to have people save money
   b. to expose people to healthy food
   c. to get people to exercise frequently
   d. to require people to eat healthy food

30. What do the administrators at Coralis assume?
   a. that people who exercise eat better
   b. that people who exercise do better work
   c. that people who exercise follow orders
   d. that people who exercise are happier

31. What is probably a major factor that led company administrators to decide to build their own gym rather than using an outside one?
   a. The company gym will have more classes than the private gym.
   b. The company gym will have more facilities than the private gym.
   c. The company gym will be less expensive for the company in the long run.
   d. The company gym will be larger than the private gym.

Questions 32 through 37 refer to the following excerpt from a short story.

What Will He Do?

"Nothing's going right . . . absolutely nothing," Jim said under his breath as he looked at his car. It was the third time this week it wouldn't start, which meant he
(5)   would be late to work again. His troubles didn't end there, though. His girlfriend had just broken up with him, and he hadn't slept all night.

His father could see him from the
(10)   living room window. He thought his son's face looked like a dried prune, it was so twisted up with anger. He felt sorry for his son. He remembered how hard it had been for him when he was just out of school and
(15)   felt lost, but he didn't know how to help.

Jim walked through the door. "Hey, Dad, can you give me a ride to work? I can't get the car started—again." His father nodded and grabbed his keys.

(20)   In the car there wasn't a lot of talk, until Jim mentioned he had been to the recruiting office.

"I don't want you to go into the army,"
his father exploded. "You don't know what it
(25)   will be like. Things will start to get better.
Just give yourself some time."

"There really isn't anything here for
me. I need a change. I think the army would
help me. Teach me some skills. I could go to
(30)   college afterward."

"And what if there is no afterward?
What about that? We love you, Jim. We don't
want to lose you."

"That's just the chance I would have to
(35)   take." Jim was aware of how his parents felt.
But he wanted to do something with his life.
He didn't want to wait for something to
happen. He hadn't gotten into the school he
wanted to attend. His girlfriend was gone.
(40)   What reason was there for him to stay?

Jim took a deep breath and then started
to talk in a firm tone.

"Sorry, Dad, but I've already made my
decision. I signed up last week. I'm going to
(45)   be leaving for training in about two weeks."

Quite suddenly, his father pulled off
the road. "Jim, Jim, you did this without
talking to us. Why? Why? Your mother . . ."
and his voice trailed off. He looked down. He
(50)   didn't know what to do. Then he turned to
his son.

"We love you, Jim," he said as he
hugged him.

"I love you too, Dad. It will be all right.
(55)   I promise."

32. When does the scene in this excerpt take place?
   a. late afternoon
   b. morning
   c. midday
   d. early evening

33. Based on the information in this excerpt, how do Jim and his father's viewpoints differ?
   a. Jim feels his father is unreasonable, but his father feels that Jim is being irresponsible.
   b. Jim feels slighted by his father, and his father is bewildered by him.
   c. Jim thinks he is being realistic, and his father thinks he is rushing his decision.
   d. Jim believes his father is too idealistic, and his father feels that Jim is too opportunistic.

34. What form of figurative language does the author use when he or she says, "He thought his son's face looked like a dried prune, it was so twisted up with anger (lines 10 through 12)"?
   a. metaphor
   b. hyperbole
   c. simile
   d. personification

35. What is Jim's father's greatest fear?
   a. that Jim will do poorly in the military
   b. that Jim might be killed in action
   c. that Jim won't go to college
   d. that Jim may never straighten out

36. What does Jim's father suggest about how Jim's mother will react to the news that Jim has enlisted?
   a. She will be horrified by his decision.
   b. She will disown him if he leaves.
   c. She will try to take him out of the country.
   d. She will understand his predicament.

37. Based on the excerpt, which of the following words would the narrator most likely use to describe Jim?
   a. confused and impractical
   b. angry and spiteful
   c. cruel and determined
   d. desperate and decisive

Questions 38 through 42 refer to the following excerpt from a review.

Will He Continue to Watch the Show?

Readers, I want you to know that I am not prejudiced against women, but I can't ignore the blatant, self-serving attitude of this new television series *Housewives Revealed*. Who
(5)   cares what these women do? Who wants to know about their catty, little minds?

   Well, apparently almost everyone does because despite my dire predictions in last month's column, *Housewives Revealed* is
(10)   a smash hit, not just with middle-aged women, which might be expected, but also with the younger set and even, heaven forbid, some guys. Go figure! For me, the only reason to watch the show is to see how
(15)   low these women are willing to stoop for a bit of glory—five minutes of fame. No one's going to get any acting awards, but there will be lots of publicity. And, who knows what else it will garner?

(20)   The plot of the series is, simply put, loose. In fact, there is no plot of any consequence, just endless comments and nitpicking among the team of four women who pretend they can act. Well, they do act
(25)   and react, all in their own way, which varies little from who they actually are. The acting is something of a joke.

   The tryouts for the coveted roles were months in the making, with a huge number
(30)   of ladies seeking the prize of a part in this new production, a cross between a sitcom and reality TV. Every Tuesday night, we are allowed into the insane, little world where there is no such thing as morality or mental
(35)   courage. But so much for my ranting.

   It is a show that people want to watch. The impression is that viewers are peeking through a window watching the antics of these housewives who give such personal
(40)   glimpses into their lives that one almost feels guilty. I guess that is its appeal. So enjoy it if you wish, but I hope that someday some new series—that refresh instead of embarrass— will appear on the television networks'
(45)   schedules.

38. Which of the following best expresses the opinion of the author of the excerpt?
   a. The author believes that younger women will watch the show.
   b. The author feels that better actors should have been chosen for the show.
   c. The author is not sure that sitcoms are worth watching.
   d. The author dislikes the show but realizes that a lot of people like it.

39. Which of the following best describes the style in which the excerpt is written?
   a. lighthearted
   b. ill-tempered
   c. quiet
   d. sentimental

40. Based on the information in the excerpt, which is the best description of *Housewives Revealed*?
   a. silly and joking
   b. indecent and improvised
   c. contained and structured
   d. sincere and meaningful

41. Based on the information in the excerpt, what audience is most likely to enjoy the television show?
  a. middle-aged men who are happily married
  b. women who are in difficult relationships
  c. women with young children
  d. grandparents

42. Which of the following changes would most likely cause the reviewer to have a more favorable opinion of the television show?
  a. a well-written script
  b. more female actors
  c. a plot that ends happily
  d. more of a reality show

Questions 43 through 50 are based on the following passage.

How to Change a Flat Tire

(A)

(1) Getting a flat tire isn't much fun, but its not as bad if you know how to change a tire. (2) If you get a flat, you should slow down and pull off the road as far as you can get from traffic. (3) After you turn the engine off, put on your hazard lights, and apply your emergency break. (4) May want open your hood to indicate to passing drivers that you are stopped for repairs just in case someone wants to help you.

(B)

(5) To stabilize the car and keep it from rolling, you should place a wheel chock behind or in front of the wheel, or a large rock, depending on which way the vehicle is sloping. (6) You will find the spare tire in the trunk along with a lug nut wrench and you may or may not need to remove the hubcap, so you should check your driver's manual to see.

(C)

(7) The lug nuts hold the wheel in place and you can loosen and remove them. (8) To do so, you should place the lug nut wrench over a lug nut, turn it counterclockwise a few turns, and then loosen the nut opposite it a few turns, and so on until all of the nuts are loose. (9) Then you are ready to use the jack. (10) You can probably find it in the trunk near where the spare tire was.

(D)

(11) Follow the manual directions on where to place the jack under your car and, once it is positioned, jacking up the car slowly. (12) When it is high enough, remove all the lug nuts take the flat tire off and put the spare tire on. (13) Then put the lug nuts back on and tighten the lug nuts the same way you loosened them. (14) Finally, lower the car down slowly and remove the jack. (15) It's a good idea to take your car to a garage and have the lug nuts professionally tightened, and while you are their have them check to see if the spare is a real tire or just a temporary one, in which case you will need to buy a new tire.

43. Sentence (1): Getting a flat tire isn't much fun, but its not as bad if you know how to change a tire.

Which correction should be made to sentence (1)?
  a. change *know* to *knew*
  b. change *isn't* to *won't*
  c. remove the comma
  d. change *its* to *it's*

44. Sentence (4): <u>May want</u> open your hood to indicate to passing drivers that you are stopped for repairs just in case someone wants to help you.

Which is the best way to write the underlined portion of this sentence? If the original is the best way, choose choice **a**.

a. May want
b. You want
c. They may want to
d. You may want to

45. Sentence (5): To stabilize the car and keep it from rolling, you should place a wheel chock behind or in front of the wheel, or a large rock, depending on which way the vehicle is sloping.

Which correction should be made to sentence (5)?

a. change *stabilize* to *stabilizes*
b. change *place* to *placed*
c. remove the comma after *rolling*
d. move *or a large rock* after *wheel chock*

46. Sentence (7): The lug nuts hold the wheel in place and you can loosen and remove them.

Which revision would improve the effectiveness of sentence (7)?

a. replace sentence (7) with *The lug nuts hold the wheel in place, therefore you will have to loosen and remove them.*
b. replace sentence (7) with *Lug nuts can be removed before taking the flat off.*
c. move sentence (7) to the end of the paragraph
d. remove sentence (7)

47. Sentence (8): To do so, you should place the lug nut wrench over a lug nut, turn it counterclockwise a few turns, and <u>then loosen</u> the nut opposite it a few turns, and so on until all of the nuts are loose.

Which is the best way to write the underlined portion of this sentence? If the original is the best way, choose choice **a**.

a. then loosen
b. then loosening
c. then loosens
d. then loosened

48. Sentences (9) and (10): Then you are ready to use the jack. You can probably find it in the trunk near where the spare tire was.

The most effective combination of sentences (9) and (10) would include which group of words?

a. that you can probably
b. so that you can probably
c. and yet you can probably
d. as though you can probably

49. Sentence (11): Follow the manual directions on where to place the jack under your car and, once it is positioned, <u>jacking up the car</u> slowly.

Which is the best way to write the underlined portion of this sentence? If the original is the best way, choose choice **a**.

a. jacking up the car
b. jacked up the car
c. is jacking up the car
d. jack up the car

50. Sentence (15): It's a good idea to take your car to a garage and have the lug nuts professionally tightened, and while you are their have them check to see if the spare is a real tire or just a temporary one, in which case you will need to buy a new tire.

Which correction should be made to sentence (15)?

a. change *tightened* to *tightening*
b. change *their* to *there*
c. change *check* to *checks*
d. change *buy* to *by*

Read the following passages. Then, read the prompt and write an essay taking a stance. Use information from the passages to support your essay.

Remarks of President Barack Obama at the Signing of Stem Cell Executive Order and Scientific Integrity Presidential Memorandum, March 9, 2009 (excerpt)

"At this moment, the full promise of stem cell research remains unknown, and it should not be overstated. But scientists believe these tiny cells may have the potential to help us understand, and possibly cure, some of our most devastating diseases and conditions. To regenerate a severed spinal cord and lift someone from a wheelchair. To spur insulin production and spare a child from a lifetime of needles. To treat Parkinson's, cancer, heart disease and others that affect millions of Americans and the people who love them.

"But that potential will not reveal itself on its own. Medical miracles do not happen simply by accident. They result from painstaking and costly research—from years of lonely trial and error, much of which never bears fruit—and from a government willing to support that work. From life-saving vaccines, to pioneering cancer treatments, to the sequencing of the human genome—that is the story of scientific progress in America. When government fails to make these investments, opportunities are missed. Promising avenues go unexplored. Some of our best scientists leave for other countries that will sponsor their work. And those countries may surge ahead of ours in the advances that transform our lives.

"But in recent years, when it comes to stem cell research, rather than furthering discovery, our government has forced what I believe is a false choice between sound science and moral values. In this case, I believe the two are not inconsistent. As a person of faith, I believe we are called to care for each other and work to ease human suffering. I believe we have been given the capacity and will to pursue this research—and the humanity and conscience to do so responsibly."

Letter to the Editor
Opposing Embryonic Stem Cell Research

March 10, 2009

Dear Editor:

Funny how politicians always talk about "stem cell research" when they really mean "embryonic stem cell research." The issue of embryonic stem cell research is so much simpler than everybody is letting on. Here are the facts: if stem cells come from embryos, then you are relying on the destruction of human life to perform medical experiments. How can anyone consider this to be ethical?

Some people come up with excuses. "It's not really an embryo because it hasn't yet attached to the womb," I've heard someone say. But if life begins at conception, it doesn't really matter how old the embryo is. "Many embryos are naturally flushed out of a woman's system without ever growing into babies," someone else said. And I say, that's for God to decide . . . not scientists.

What about using embryonic stem cells from aborted fetuses? That's like using the funds from a drug operation to build a hospital. If it's wrong, it's wrong, and it doesn't matter how good your intentions are. The ends do not justify the means.

The worst part is, stem cells don't have to come from embryos. Scientists have already been using stem cells from adults for decades. They say that embryonic stem cells are more versatile and hold more potential. Well, children are better suited for climbing into mine shafts, too. Does that mean we should make children work in coal mines? To me, that doesn't sound much like progress.

Sincerely,

Jacob Feeney

Prompt

These two passages present different arguments regarding the issue of stem cell research. In your response, analyze both positions to determine which one is best supported. Use relevant and specific evidence from the passages to support your response.

Answers

1. b. Rosedale clearly states that her apartment is no place for her. There is no mention of him being a suitor.

2. a. Lily is both embarrassed and impressed by Rosedale's words. She has never seen him act like this, and she blushes.

3. d. The reader should infer that Lily is head-strong; she is proud and independent. No mention is made of her education, and she can't be considered needy.

4. a. Rosedale clearly states that the idea of Lily's working is outrageous. He feels she is above having to work. His actions indicate how emotional he is about this.

5. b. Rosedale's words and his manner of speaking both point to a sense of bluntness and deter-mination in his dealing with Lily. He is cer-tainly not acting like a shy man.

6. d. Rosedale cannot talk calmly; the tone of the passage is indeed quite intense, and Lily has never seen him like this before. This is the best description of the excerpt's mood.

7. b. The passage suggests that Lily did not want to have Rosedale pursue her when Rosedale says, "I know it's none of my business—you've let me understand that often enough."

8. c. Choice **c** is correct because *that* agrees with the antecedent *position*, which is a thing and not a person. Choice **a** changes the verb to an incorrect past tense. Choice **b** inserts an unnecessary comma. Choice **d** incorrectly capitalizes *newspaper*.

9. a. Choice **a** is correct. This creates a sentence out of a fragment by adding the subject *I*. Choice **b** has an incorrect verb form. Choice **c** also adds a subject, but this subject does not agree with the verb phrase *have been involved*. Choice **d** has a verb that does not agree with its singular subject.

10. d. Choice **d** is correct. All parts of proper names should be capitalized. The other choices do not capitalize the entire name of the school, so they are incorrect.

11. b. There are two words misspelled in this sentence. The term *meat* refers to food and should be replaced by *meet*, which means *get together*. The term *farther* refers to distance; the proper term would be *further*, which means *additionally*. Choice **b** is correct. Choices **a**, **c**, and **d** all change verbs unnecessarily.

12. a. Choice **a** is correct since this verb agrees with the subject, and the comma after *people* is unneeded. Choice **b** is incorrect because there is no reason for a possessive form of the noun. Choice **c** inserts another unnecessary comma. Choice **d** has an incorrect verb form and an incorrect pronoun.

13. c. Choice **c** is correct. Items in lists need to be separated by commas. Choice **a** has no comma separating the items. Choice **b** has one comma but needs another between *phone number* and *email address*. Choice **d** misuses a semicolon.

14. c. The song reminds Diana of faraway places like Kashmir, and the cicadas are the first things she listens for when she comes to Port Said, so they both suggest faraway places. They certainly do not bring up frightening emotions, and there is nothing in the text to suggest the other possibilities, either.

15. a. The mood is reflective as Diana remembers past travels and talks about beauty and color. There is no sorrow in her thoughts. She doesn't seem quarrelsome, either.

16. a. Diana is passionate about music, art, and beautiful clothes, and she shows her independence when she challenges Arbuth with uplifted eyes.

17. d. Arbuth questions Diana about what she has said about herself—that she is not emotional—when he believes she is being emotional about the song. He may think she is very feminine, but this isn't said in the excerpt. He doesn't appear to think she is a difficult woman, either.

18. b. Diana is presented as a person of some wealth who travels a great deal and enjoys being in wild places; she looks forward to being in the desert.

19. d. Choice **d** is correct because it smoothly combines the ideas in both sentences. Choice **a** changes the meaning of the two sentences, as does choice **c**. Choice **b** confuses the meaning of the sentence.

20. d. Choice **d** is correct because *weighing* is a parallel verb form to the earlier verb, *measuring*. Choice **a** inserts an incorrect homonym for *their*. Choice **b** incorrectly changes the verb to a plural form. Choice **c** changes the verb to an incorrect singular form.

21. d. Choice **d** is correct because the verb agrees with the subject. Choice **a** uses a verb with an incorrect past tense. Choice **b** is incorrect because it incorrectly substitutes an adjective for the adverb. Choice **c** changes the meaning of the sentence.

22. d. Choice **d** is correct because *since* makes the comma splice a compound sentence. Choice **a** changes a correct verb form into an incorrect one. Choice **b** inserts an unnecessary comma. Choice **c** would create a run-on sentence.

23. c. Choice **c** is correct because this verb is in past tense, which is when the action took place. Choice **a** uses an incorrect future tense for the verb. Choice **b** changes the meaning of the sentence. Choice **d** uses an inappropriate past tense verb that also does not agree with the subject.

24. a. Choice **a** is correct because this change uses the correct homonym for the context of the sentence, which is a word that means *understanding* and not a word that means *has never been used*. Choice **b** creates a possessive noun where none is needed. Choice **c** changes a correct past tense form of the verb into an incorrect present tense. Choice **d** uses an incorrect verb form.

25. d. Choice **d** is correct because *its* does not agree with the antecedent *manatees* while the plural possessive *their* does. Choice **a** is wrong because it inserts an unnecessary comma. Choice **b** changes a verb that agrees with the subject to one that does not. *Taino* is the proper name of a group of people, so that must be capitalized, making choice **c** wrong.

26. a. Coralis feels that the program will result in an increase in employee production because fit employees will work better. This can be seen in lines 39 through 41, where the text states that improving employee fitness "will doubtless have a positive impact on employee production."

27. a. The program will help those who have trouble staying on a diet by rewarding them with tokens that can be used for low-fat meals, fruits, and vegetables.

28. c. An executive who works odd hours would probably use a personal trainer since he or she probably can't attend the regularly scheduled exercise classes. A salesperson who travels a lot will not be around that much, so he or she might not be available for personal training, although it might be argued that when the salesperson is around, he or she might opt for personal training. Even so, choice **c** is the better answer.

29. b. The use of tokens will allow people to try foods for free that they might not choose otherwise. That may or may not make them healthier, too, but that is not necessarily the main goal of the program.

30. b. The assumption of the administration is that fit employees will work harder and be more productive because they will feel better and have more energy.

31. c. Outsourcing exercise facilities will probably cost more over time than having a gym on-site, so this is the best answer. The other choices are not supported by the text.

32. b. The excerpt says that Jim needed to get to work and that he did not sleep the night before. This supports the answer that the scene takes place in the morning.

33. c. By what happens in the scene, the reader can figure out that Jim is determined to make his own decisions, while his father would prefer it if Jim thought about it for a while.

34. c. The author is using a simile. The use of the word *like* indicates this. The son's face was contorted with anger, which reminded the father of the image of a dried prune.

35. b. Jim's father does not want to lose his son; he could be killed in action. There is no reason to believe that the father fears Jim will not straighten his life out.

36. a. The mother will be horrified by Jim's decision to enter the army, but there is nothing in the text to support the idea that she would disown him. Her horror that he might be killed illustrates her affection for her son.

37. d. Jim is desperate because his girlfriend left him, and he is decisive in his choice to join the army, which he thinks will give him a new start in life.

38. d. The author does not like the show but accepts the reality that it is a hit show that people want to watch. The other choices are not supported by the review.

39. b. The author's tone is quite ill-tempered and not tolerant at all of the television series. There is nothing sentimental or lighthearted about it.

40. b. The author believes that viewing people's regular lives is like peering into someone's window, which is indecent and inappropriate. Because there is no real script, all dialogue is improvised in the sense that the women decide what they are going to say as events happen. The author is not saying that the show is meaningful.

41. b. Women who are in difficult relationships will most likely be drawn to this show because it will offer them some respite to see actors nit-picking on TV.

42. a. The author would appreciate a well-written script rather than a show that is basically scriptless. This is the best answer.

43. d. Choice **d** is correct. The sentence calls for a contraction of *it is* and not the possessive form of *its*. Choices **a** and **b** insert incorrect verb forms. Choice **c** removes a comma that is needed before the conjunction in a compound sentence.

44. d. Choice **d** is correct because it includes the missing subject, making the fragment a complete sentence, as well as the preposition *to*, which is needed in front of the verb *open*. Choice **a** lacks a subject, and choice **b** lacks the preposition. Choice **c** uses the wrong pronoun for the subject.

45. d. Choice **d** is correct because the phrase modifies *wheel chock*, not *wheel*. Choices **a** and **b** replace correct verbs with incorrect ones. Choice **c** removes a needed comma after an opening clause.

46. a. Choice **a** is correct because the changes that are made to the sentence create a connection between the lug nuts and why they need to be removed. Choice **b** does not create a connection between them. Moving sentence (7) wouldn't help the organization or the sentence; therefore, choice **c** is incorrect. Sentence (7) has valuable information and should not be deleted, so choice **d** is also incorrect.

47. a. Choice **a** is correct. This verb form parallels the earlier verb *turn*, and so it is correct. The other choices use incorrect verb forms and do not parallel the earlier verb.

48. a. Choice **a** is correct. These words join both ideas in the sentences smoothly. The other choices change the meaning of the sentences and are not appropriate ways to join the two sentences.

49. d. Choice **d** is the correct verb tense and form for this sentence. All the other choices have either a wrong tense or form, or do not agree with the subject, which is understood as *you*.

50. b. Choice **b** is correct because it inserts the proper homonym, a word that means *that place*. Choice **a** has an incorrect verb form, as does choice **c**. Choice **d** inserts an incorrect homonym of *buy* that doesn't fit the meaning of the sentence, which calls for a word that means *to purchase*.

Extended Response

For this prompt, the two sides of the issue—stem cell research—are framed very differently. This can make it harder to compare the passages directly, but can also make it easier to analyze the differences between the two arguments. For example, President Obama's speech focuses on the potential benefits of stem cell research. He even offers specific examples of how this research might help those in need. However, these examples are only potential scenarios, since there is no guarantee that stem cell research will succeed in solving these problems. Obama also urges people to reconcile their religious beliefs with their own sense of kindness and cooperation to others. By contrast, the letter to the editor focuses at first on an appeal to authority—in this case, God—to shut down arguments in favor of embryonic stem cell research. This can be a powerful form of argument, but it relies on an authority figure rather than specific examples or data for support. The letter makes a comparison between stem cells and money acquired through drug dealing, and this is a great specific example to note in the extended response. The letter to the editor also takes the argument about embryonic stem cells' versatility and potential and applies the same argument to child labor; some might find this argument compelling, while others might consider it to be absurd. In either case, the purpose of the extended response is not to choose the "right" side—the purpose is to effectively analyze the issues and arguments presented in the passages.

APPENDIX: PREFIXES, SUFFIXES, AND WORD ROOTS

Prefixes

The following table lists the most common English language prefixes, their meanings, and several examples of words with each prefix.

PREFIX	MEANING	EXAMPLES
a-, an-	not, without	atypical, anarchy, amorphous
ab-, abs-	from, away, off	abnormal, abduct, abscond
ante-	prior to, in front of, before	antedate, antecedent, antebellum
ant-, anti-	opposite, opposing, against	antidote, antagonist, antipathy
bi-	two, twice	bisect, bilateral, bicameral
circum-	around, about, on all sides	circumference, circumnavigate, circumspect
co-, com-, con-	with, together, jointly cooperate	coexist, community, consensus
contra-	against, contrary, contrasting	contradict, contraindication
counter-	contrary, opposite or opposing; complementary	counterclockwise, countermeasure, counterpart
de-	do the opposite or reverse of; remove from, reduce	deactivate, dethrone, detract
dis-	away from, apart, reversal, not	disperse, dismiss, disinterested
du-, duo-	two	duo, duet, duality
ex-	out, out of, away from	expel, exclaim, exorbitant
in-, il-, im-, ir-	in, into, within	induct, impart, inculcate, illuminate, irradiate

(Continued)

PREFIX	MEANING	EXAMPLES
in-, il-, im-, ir-	not	invariable, incessant, illicit, inept, impervious, irreverent
inter-	between, among, within	intervene, interact, intermittent
intra-	within, during	intramural, intravenous
intro-	in, into, within	introvert, introduction
mal-	bad, abnormal, evil, wrong	malfunction, malpractice, malign
mis-	bad, wrong, ill	misspell, miscreant, misanthrope
mono-	one, single, alone	monologue, monogamy, monocle
multi-	many	multiple, multimillionaire, multifarious
neo-	new, recent, a new form of	neologism, neonatal, neophyte
non-	not	nonconformist, nonentity, nonchalant
over-	exceeding, surpassing, excessive	overabundance, overstimulate
poly-	many, much	polyester, polytechnic, polyglot
post-	after, subsequent, later (than); behind	postpone, postpartum, postoperative, posterior
pre-	before	precaution, precede, presage
pro-	earlier, before, prior to; in front of; for, supporting, in place of; forward	proceed, proclivity, profess, projecting
pseudo-	false, fake	pseudonym, pseudoscience
re-	back, again	recall, reconcile, rescind
semi-	half, partly, incomplete	semiannual, semiconscious
sub-	under, beneath, below	subconscious, subdue, subjugate
super-	above, over, exceeding	superhero, superficial, supercilious
trans-	across, beyond, through	transmit, translate, translucent
tri-	three, thrice	triangle, tricycle, triumvirate
un-	not	unable, uninterested, unorthodox
uni-	one	uniform, unilateral, universal

Suffixes

The following table lists the most common English language suffixes, their meanings, and several examples of words with each suffix.

Noun Endings

SUFFIX	MEANING	EXAMPLES
-age	action or process; house or place of; state, rank	drainage, orphanage, marriage
-al	action or process	rehearsal, disposal, reversal
-an, -ian	of or relating to; a person specializing in	guardian, pediatrician, historian, American
-ance, -ence	action or process; state of	adolescence, benevolence, renaissance
-ancy, -ency	quality or state	agency, vacancy, latency
-ant, -ent	one that performs, promotes, or causes an action; being in a specified state or condition	disinfectant, dissident, miscreant
-ary	thing belonging to or connected with	adversary, dignitary, library
-cide	killer, killing	suicide, pesticide, homicide
-cy	action or practice; state of, quality of	democracy, legitimacy, supremacy
-er, -or	person or thing that is, does, or performs	builder, foreigner, sensor
-ion, -sion, -tion	act or process; state or condition	attraction, persecution, denunciation, evasion, contagion
-ism	act, practice, or process; state or doctrine of	critism, anachronism, imperialism
-ist	one who (performs, makes, produces, believes, etc.)	anarchist, feminist, imperialist
-ity	quality, state, or degree	clarity, amity, veracity
-ment	action or process; result, object, means, or agent of an action or process	entertainment, embankment, amazement
-ness	state, condition, quality, or degree	happiness, readiness, goodness
-ology	doctrine, theory, or science; oral or written expression	biology, theology, eulogy
-or	condition, activity	candor, valor, succor
-sis	process or action	diagnosis, dialysis, metamorphosis
-ure	act or process; office or function	exposure, legislature, censure
-y	state, condition, quality; activity or place of business	laundry, empathy, anarchy

Adjective Endings

SUFFIX	MEANING	EXAMPLES
-able, -ible	capable or worthy of; tending or liable to	flammable, culpable, inscrutable, invisible
-al, -ial, -ical	having the quality of; of, relating to, or characterized by	educational, peripheral, ephemeral, menial, hysterical
-an, -ian	one who is or does; related to, characteristic of	human, American, agrarian
-ant, -ent	performing (a specific action) or being (in a specified condition)	important, incessant, preeminent
-ful	full of; having the qualities of; tending or liable to	helpful, peaceful, wistful
-ic	pertaining or relating to; having the quality of	fantastic, chronic, archaic
-ile	tending to or capable of	fragile, futile, servile
-ish	having the quality of	Swedish, bookish, squeamish
-ive	performing or tending toward (an action); having the nature of	sensitive, cooperative, pensive
-less	without, lacking; unable to act or be acted on (in a specified way)	endless, fearless, listless
-ose, -ous	full of, having the qualities of, relating to	adventurous, glorious, egregarious, bellicose
-y	characterized by, full of; tending or inclined to	sleepy, cursory, desultory

Verb Endings

SUFFIX	MEANING	EXAMPLES
-ate	to make, to cause to be or become	violate, tolerate, exacerbate, emanate
-en	to cause to be or have; to come to be or have	quicken, lengthen, frighten
-fy	to make	beautify, electrify, rectify
-ize	to cause to be or become; to bring about	colonize, plagiarize, synchronize

Word Roots

The following table lists the most common word roots, their meanings, and several examples of words with those roots.

There are more than 150 roots here, but don't be intimidated by the length of this list. Break it down into manageable chunks of 10 to 20 roots, and memorize them section by section. Remember that you use words with these roots every day.

ROOT	MEANING	EXAMPLES
ac, acr	sharp, bitter	acid, acute, acrimonious
act, ag	to do, to drive, to force, to lead	agent, enact, agitate
ad, al	to, toward, near	adjacent, adhere, allure
al, all, alter	other, another	alternative, alias, alien
amb	to go, to walk	ambulatory, preamble, ambush
amb, amph	both, more than one, around	ambiguous, ambivalent, amphitheater
anim	life, mind, soul, spirit	unanimous, animosity, equanimity
anni, annu, enni	year	annual, anniversary, perennial
anthro, andr	man, human	anthropology, android, misanthrope
apo	away	apology, apocalypse, apotheosis
apt, ept	skill, fitness, ability	adapt, adept, inept
arch, arche, archi, archy	chief, principal, ruler, beginning	hierarchy, monarch, anarchy, archetype
auto	self	automatic, autonomy, automaton
bel, bell	war	rebel, belligerent, antebellum
ben, bon	good	benefit, benevolent, bonus
cad, cid	to fall, to happen by chance	accident, coincidence, cascade
cant, cent, chant	to sing	chant, enchant, recant, accent
cap, capit, cip, cipit	head, headlong	capital, principal, capitulate, precipitous
cap, cip, cept	to take, to get	capture, intercept, emancipate
card, cord, cour	heart	encourage, cardiac, discord
carn	flesh	carnivore, reincarnation, carnage
cast, chast	cut	caste, chastise, castigate
cede, ceed, cess	to go, to yield, to stop	exceed, concede, incessant

(Continued)

ROOT	MEANING	EXAMPLES
centr	center	central, concentric, eccentric
cern, cert, cret, crim, crit	to separate, to judge, to distinguish, to decide	ascertain, critique, discern, discretion, incriminate
chron	time	chronic, chronology, synchronize
cis	to cut	scissors, precise, incisive
cla, clo, clu	shut, close	closet, enclose, preclude, enclave
claim, clam	to shout, to cry out	exclaim, proclaim, clamor
cli, clin	to lean toward, bend	decline, recline, proclivity
cour, cur	running, a course	recur, incursion, cursory, discourse
cracy, crat	to govern	democracy, autocracy, bureaucrat
cre, cres, cret	to grow	creation, increase, increment, crescent, accretion
cred	to believe, to trust	incredible, credit, incredulous
cryp	hidden	crypt, cryptic, cryptography
cub, cumb	to lie down	succumb, incubate, incumbent
culp	blame	culprit, culpable, exculpate
dem	people	democracy, epidemic, pandemic
di, dia	apart, through	dialogue, diatribe, dichotomy
dic, diet, dit	to say, to tell, to use words	predict, dictionary, indict, indicate, indite
dign	worth	dignity, indignant
doc	to teach	doctor, indoctrinate, docile
dog, dox	opinion	dogma, orthodox, paradox
dol	suffer, pain	condolence, indolence, dolorous
don, dot, dow	to give	donate, endow, anecdote
dub	doubt	dubious, indubitable, dubiety
duc, duct	to lead	conduct, induct, conducive
dur	hard	endure, durable, obdurate
dys	faulty, abnormal	dysfunctional, dystopia, dyslexia
epi	among, upon	epidemic, epigram, epigraph
equ	equal, even	equation, equanimity, equivocate
err	to wander	error, erratic
esce	becoming	adolescent, coalesce, acquiesce
eu	good, well	euphoria, eulogy, euthanasia
fab, fam	speak	fable, famous, affable
fac, fic, fig, fait, felt, fy	to do, to make	fiction, factory, figment, surfeit, clarify

(Continued)

ROOT	MEANING	EXAMPLES
fer	to bring, to carry, to bear	offer, transfer, proliferate
ferv	to boil, to bubble	fervor, fervid, effervescent
fid	faith, trust	confide, fidelity, infidel
fin	end	final, finite, affinity
flag, flam	to burn	flammable, inflammatory, flagrant
flect, flex	to bend	deflect, reflect, flexible
flu, fluc, flux	to flow	fluid, fluctuation, superfluous, influx
fore	before	foresight, forestall, forebear
fort	chance	fortune, fortunate, fortuitous
fra, frac, frag, fring	to break	fracture, fraction, infringe, fragile
fus	to pour	confuse, infusion, diffuse
gen	birth, creation, race; kind	genetics, homogenous, generous
gn, gno	to know	ignore, recognize, incognito
grad, gres	to step	progress, aggressive, digress, gradual
grat	pleasing	grateful, gratitude, ingratiate
her, hes	to stick	cohere, adherent, inherent, hesitate
(h)etero	different, other	heterosexual, heterogeneous, heterodox
(h)om	same	homogeneous, homonym, anomaly
hyper	over, excessive	hyperactive, hyperextend, hyperbole
id	one's own	idiom, idiosyncrasy, ideology
ject	to throw, to throw down	eject, dejected, conjecture
join, junct, juxt	to meet, to join	joint, junction, juxtapose
jur	to swear	jury, perjury, abjure
lect, leg	to select, to choose	election, select, eclectic, legislate
lev	lift, light, rise	elevator, lever, alleviate
loc, log, loqu	word, speech	dialogue, eloquent, loquacious, elocution
luc, lum, lus	light	illustrate, lucid, luminous.
lud, lus	to play	illusion, elude, allude
lav, lug, lut, luv	to wash	lavatory, dilute, deluge, alluvial
mag, maj, max	big	magnify, major, maximum
man	hand	manual, manufacture, manifest
min	small	minute, diminish, minutiae
min	to project, to hang over	prominent, imminent, preeminent
mit	to send	transmit, remit, intermittent

(Continued)

ROOT	MEANING	EXAMPLES
mon, monit	to warn	monitor, admonish, remonstrate
morph	shape	amorphous, metamorphosis, anthropomorphic
mor, mort	death	immortal, morbid, moratorium
mut	change	mutate, immutable, permutation
nom	rule, order	economy, taxonomy, autonomy
nat, nas, nai	to be born	native, nascent, renaissance
nec, nic, noc, nox	harm, death	innocent, noxious, innocuous, necrosis, pernicious
nom, nym, noun, nown	name	nominate, homonym, nominal, pronoun, renown
nounc, nunc	to announce	pronounce, denounce, annunciation
nov, neo	new	novice, novel, neophyte
ob, oc, of, op	toward, to, against, completely, over	object, obstruct, obsequious, occupy, oppose, offend
omni	all	omnipresent, omnipotent. omniscient
pac, peas	peace	pacify, appease, pacifier
pan	all, everyone	panorama, pandemic, panacea
par	equal	disparate, parity
para	next to, beside	parallel, paragon, paradox
pas, pat, path	feeling, suffering, disease	passionate, antipathy, apathetic
pau, po, pov, pu	few, little, poor	poverty, pauper, impoverish, puerile
ped	child, education	pediatrician, encyclopedia, pedantic
ped, pod	foot	pedestrian, expedite, podiatry
pen, pun	to pay	penalty, punishment, penance
pend, pens	to hang, to weigh, to pay	depend, compensate, pensive
per	completely, wrong	perplex, permeate, pervade, perversion
pen	around	perimeter, peripheral, peripatetic
per	to go, to seek, to strive	compete, petition, impetuous
phil	love	philosophy, philanthropy, bibliophile
phon, phone	sound	telephone, homophone, cacophony
plac	to please	placid, placebo, complacent
pie	to fill	complete, deplete, plethora
plex, plic, ply	to fold, to twist, to tangle, to bend	complex, comply, implicit

(Continued)

ROOT	MEANING	EXAMPLES
pon, pos, pound	to put, to place	expose, component, juxtapose, impound
port	to carry	import, portable, importune
prehend, pris, prise	to take, to get, to seize	surprise, apprehend, reprisal
pro	much, for, a lot	proliferate, profuse, proselytize
prob	to prove, to test	probe, probation, reprobate
pug	to fight	repugnant, pugnacious, impugn
punc, pung, poign	to point, to prick	puncture, punctilious, pungent, poignant
que, quis	to seek	inquisitive, conquest, query
qui	quiet	tranquil, acquiesce
rid, ris	to laugh	riddle, ridiculous, derision
rog	to ask	interrogate, surrogate, abrogate
sacr, sanct, secr	sacred	sacrament, sanction, consecrate
sol, sault, sult	to leap, to jump	assault, insolent, desultory
sci	to know	conscious, science, omniscient
scribe, scrip	to write	scribble, circumscribe, prescription
se	apart	separate, segregate, seditious
sec, sequ	to follow	consecutive sequel, obsequious
sed, sess, sid	to sit, to be still, to plan, to plot	subside, assiduous, dissident, sedentary, session
sens, sent	to feel, to be aware	sense, sentiment, dissent
sol	to loosen, to free	dissolve, resolution, dissolution
spec, spic, spit	to look, to see	perspective, speculation, circumspect, conspicuous, despite
sta, ste, sti	to stand, to be in place	static, obstinate, steadfast
sua	smooth	suave, persuade, dissuade
tac, tic	to be silent	tacit, reticent, taciturn
tain, ten, tent, tin	to hold	detain, sustain, tenacious, detention, continue
tend, tens, tent, tenu	to stretch, to thin	extend, tenson, tenuous, intent
the, theo	god	atheist, theology, apotheosis
tract	to drag, to pull, to draw	attract, detract, tractable
us, ut	to use	abuse, utility, usurp
ven, vent	to come, to move toward	convene, venture, intervene

Using the codes below, you'll be able to log in and access additional online practice materials!

Your free online practice access codes are:
FVEK7A1FQR577I5MUR27
FVE1QR0154KH3IYKEKO4
FVE52TXJKC701H42U8H3

Follow these simple steps to redeem your codes:

• Go to **www.learningexpresshub.com/affiliate** and have your access codes handy.

If you're a new user:

• Click the **New user? Register here** button and complete the registration form to create your account and access your products.
• Be sure to enter your unique access codes only once. If you have multiple access codes, you can enter them all—just use a comma to separate each code.
• The next time you visit, simply click the **Returning user? Sign in** button and enter your username and password.
• Do not re-enter previously redeemed access codes. Any products you previously accessed are saved in the **My Account** section on the site. Entering a previously redeemed access code will result in an error message.

If you're a returning user:

• Click the **Returning user? Sign in** button, enter your username and password, and click **Sign In**.
• You will automatically be brought to the **My Account** page to access your products.
• Do not re-enter previously redeemed access codes. Any products you previously accessed are saved in the **My Account** section on the site. Entering a previously redeemed access code will result in an error message.

If you're a returning user with new access codes:

• Click the **Returning user? Sign in** button, enter your username, password, and new access codes, and click **Sign In**.
• If you have multiple access codes, you can enter them all—just use a comma to separate each code.
• Do not re-enter previously redeemed access codes. Any products you previously accessed are saved in the **My Account** section on the site. Entering a previously redeemed access code will result in an error message.

If you have any questions, please contact LearningExpress Customer Support at LXHub@LearningExpressHub .com. All inquiries will be responded to within a 24-hour period during our normal business hours: 9:00 A.M.– 5:00 P.M. Eastern Time. Thank you!

Mount Laurel Library
100 Walt Whitman Avenue
Mount Laurel, NJ 08054-9539
856-234-7319
www.mtlaurel.lib.nj.us